This book works because of Christ,
who is the source of virtuous values,
and because of the integrity of the messenger.
Stuart Briscoe remains a man of constant godly values
over the long haul.
His presentations and focused discussions
will probe each of us to the heart
of our ethical assumptions.
ART GAY
president, World Relief Corporation

Our lives are filled with choices.
In his unique and wonderful way,
Stuart Briscoe helps us prioritize those choices
and to focus with passion and compassion
on the choices that matter most.
This wonderful book should be
of help and encouragement to everyone
who wants to do the will of God.
PAUL A. CEDAR
president, Evangelical Free Church of America

CHOICES
FOR A
Lifetime

Determining the Values
That Will Shape
Your Future

STUART
BRISCOE

 Tyndale House
Publishers, Inc.
Wheaton, Illinois

Published in association with the literary agency of Alive Communications, Inc., 1465 Kelly Johnson Blvd., Suite 320, Colorado Springs, CO 80920.

Scripture quotations are taken from the *Holy Bible,* New International Version®. Copyright © 1973, 1978, 1984 by International Bible Society. Used by permission of Zondervan Publishing House. All rights reserved. The "NIV" and "New International Version" trademarks are registered in the United States Patent and Trademark Office by International Bible Society. Use of either trademark requires permission of International Bible Society.

Library of Congress Cataloging-in-Publication Data

Briscoe, D. Stuart.
  Choices for a lifetime: determining the values that will shape your future / Stuart Briscoe.
      p.   cm.
  Includes bibliographical references.
  ISBN 0-8423-1784-8
  1. Christian ethics.   2. Christian life.   3. Values.   I. Title.
  BJ1251.B75   1995
  241—dc20   95-9294

Printed in the United States of America

00 99 98 97 96 95
8   7   6   5   4   3   2

ACKNOWLEDGMENTS

Special thanks to the staff at Tyndale House, especially Ron Beers and Ken Petersen, with whom the project was first discussed; and Vinita Wright, whose editorial pencil is always to the point; Rick Christian of Alive Communications, who makes good things happen; and my daughter-in-law, Debra, who, in addition to caring for her pastor husband and four lively kids, found time to type endlessly and accurately.

To the
long-suffering congregation of
ELMBROOK CHURCH
Brookfield, Wisconsin,
who share my concerns,
listen to my sermons,
laugh at my jokes,
and generally make ministry a joy.
The Elmbrook people
heard these chapters
in sermonic form,
so they will probably not buy this book
and accordingly never see
this dedication.

CONTENTS

ONE

VALUES ARE VITAL

THERE once was a young preacher who was called to his first pastorate in a traditional church in Kentucky. He began his ministry on the first Sunday by preaching against smoking. At the end of the service the elders came up to him and said, "Young man, you must realize that a third of your congregation make their money growing tobacco."

"Oh," he said, "I didn't realize that."

They said, "Well, just bear that in mind in the future."

So the next week he preached against drinking. The elders promptly informed him, "Young man, you have to realize that in this county a third of the people distill whiskey."

"Oh," he said, "I didn't realize that."

"Well, you do now," they responded ominously.

The third week he preached against gambling. The elders said, "Young man, this is Kentucky. A third of your congregation raise thoroughbred race horses."

"Oh," he said, "I never even thought about that."

So the fourth week, finally getting the message, he preached on the dangers inherent in deep-sea diving in international waters!

Although he was quite right in asserting that drinking, smoking, and gambling have negative effects on health and well-being, this young man took the way of discretion and limited his remarks to truth that was palatable, politically correct—and irrelevant. Now that may be a smart course of action for a young pastor with job security on his mind, but it does add fuel to the flames of criticism that flicker around the church these days. The church of Jesus Christ is accused of being irrelevant to the way ordinary people go about their lives.

Take, for example, Nicols Fox's article entitled, "What Are Our Real Values?"

> Who makes the rules these days that determine how our society is going to work—the code of ethics behind the laws that determines our values and decides how we are going to live together in community? It isn't the churches. It's not so much that their moral leadership is being ignored as that, to a great extent, they've abdicated the role. Collectively they seem to exude the same relativism and insecurity about right and wrong as the rest of us. (*Newsweek,* 13 Feb. 1989)

Ms. Fox rightly assumes that society should "work," and for that to happen society needs to maintain certain rules and values. They need to come from somewhere; apparently, in her opinion and that of many others, the church has failed to do the job.

Who Can Restore Society's Values?
So if the church isn't establishing the values society needs, who is?

The politicians?
Is it possible that the politicians could succeed where their ecclesiastical counterparts have failed? Could they perhaps

instill the values our society needs so desperately? At their convention in Houston in August 1992, the Republicans spoke loud and long on the subject of "traditional family values." Yet in the November election they were rejected by the voters, ejected from the White House, and they landed dejected in the political outhouse.

THE CHURCH OF JESUS CHRIST IS ACCUSED OF BEING IRRELEVANT TO THE WAY ORDINARY PEOPLE GO ABOUT THEIR LIVES.

Columnist and political commentator Meg Greenfield spent some quality time brooding over why the "hard edged GOP family values blast of August" failed to deliver when it was time to cast a ballot. Her conclusion:

> Most of us have picked and chosen our way individually among all this, [and] have had our own personal struggles over what we can accept and what we cannot and have created our own individual equilibrium. . . . It is hardly any wonder that people were so offended by the original Republican effort to scare them back to where they had been and so inhospitable to speechmaking that politicized and vulgarized this subject known as "Family values." (*Newsweek*, 14 Sept. 1992)

Irving Kristol, writing in the *Wall Street Journal*, was even more emphatic:

Nor is there much hope to be found among politicians who stand to gain little, and lose much, by confronting the powerful forces that are so easily mobilized against the political sponsorship of "family values.". . . They will always have more urgent and less controversial problems to cope with. (7 Dec. 1992)

So, if Ms. Greenfield is right that the public is not open to being lectured by politicians about values, or if Mr. Kristol's opinion is correct that the politicians are too afraid of venturing into a values minefield, it looks as if there won't be much help coming from our political resources.

The educational system?
Can we expect more from the educational establishment? Many people have given up on this idea. Christina Hoff Sommers, after teaching ethics at the university level for fifteen years, is convinced that there is something fundamentally wrong in the American classroom. She said, "We may be one of the few societies incapable of passing on its moral teachings to young people."

She went on to say that when it comes to moral education it is as if "we've forgotten several thousand years of civilization—the great moral, religious, and philosophical traditions" ("How to Teach Right and Wrong," *Christianity Today,* 13 Dec. 1993).

It's not that our educators are unmindful of the need for character development in our younger generation. Their difficulties seem to arise from an almost religious zeal to protect the state from invasion by the church, and a corresponding enthusiasm for scrupulously avoiding any form of moral teaching that could be a form of "brainwashing." Many educators seem to have arrived at a strange compromise: to teach something called social morality without the embarrassment of having to teach private morality—as if the two can be successfully divorced. This, as Dr. Sommers pointed out, allows students to "debate abortion, euthanasia, capital punishment, DNA research and the ethics of transplant surgery while they learn almost nothing about private decency, honesty, personal responsibility, or honor."

The irony of the situation was highlighted when more than half the students in a class on ethics taught by a teacher who objected to Dr. Sommers's position were caught cheating!

> "WE MAY BE ONE OF THE FEW SOCIETIES INCAPABLE OF PASSING ON ITS MORAL TEACHINGS TO YOUNG PEOPLE."

The media?
To whom then can we turn for help? Which of our remaining great institutions can come to the aid of a society that acknowledges the deterioration of its culture? Why not the media? After all, this is the age of multimedia—it hits us at every turn—and no one knows the full extent to which we are affected by the messages conveyed through the media. Michael Medved, an outspoken critic of Hollywood and its relentless grip on entertainment media, wrote:

> The entertainment industry no longer reflects the values of most American families. For instance, in our private lives, we deplore violence and feel little sympathy for the criminals who perpetrate it, but movies revel in graphic brutality, glorifying sadistic characters who treat killing as a joke. And nearly all parents want to convey to their children the importance

of self-discipline, hard work, and decent manners, but the entertainment media celebrates [sic] vulgar behavior, contempt for all authority and gutter language—which is inserted even in "family fare" where it is least expected. ("Is Hollywood Destroying Our Values?" *Hemispheres*, Oct. 1992)

Citing an entertainer who is a huge success, namely Madonna, a.k.a. "The Material Girl," Armstrong Williams in a "Comment" column in *USA Today* wrote scathingly:

Her videos are so raunchy that MTV can't air them and MTV will air anything short of human sacrifice. The synonym of "material" is superficial, which sums up her contrived persona . . . yet her records sell because buyers don't know better. . . . Meanwhile songs with values don't get sung, and entertainers truly worthy of being icons remain unappreciated. Bad drives out good, leaving Madonna's tawdry example as one of the leading shapers of today's culture such as it is. (21 Oct. 1992)

Some people are asking the honest question: If this is so, why do we still watch the movies and listen to the music? Could it be that there is a kind of schizophrenia at work here, whereby the higher, nobler part of us desires the values and the lower, ignoble part responds to the countervalues it outwardly deplores? Nicols Fox, in the article cited earlier, seems to think so:

The trouble is, real American values are expressed not by what we say we wish for, but by what we really do. . . . Perhaps the best indicator of what we really are is what we spend our money on or what we watch on television. Look at what we read. Look at what we choose to do with our spare time. That's what we value.

So let's see if we're getting a clear picture here. There is general consensus that our society is in trouble, that our culture is wearing thin. Commentators from the Right and the Left at last agree on something! The problem appears to be related to a lack of core values or beliefs that will affect behavior in a positive way. But who is to teach these principles? The various opinions suggest that the church doesn't teach them, media won't teach them, education can't teach them, and politics dare not teach them. So where do we go from here?

> THERE IS GENERAL
> CONSENSUS THAT OUR
> SOCIETY IS IN TROUBLE,
> THAT OUR CULTURE IS
> WEARING THIN.

Poverty of Values, Lack of Models
Let's go to southern California. The year was 1992, and the then vice president of the United States, Dan Quayle, was addressing the faithful in what turned out to be an unsuccessful attempt to get reelected. In his speech he made a connection between the recent terrifying rioting in Los Angeles and what he called a "poverty of values." During the course of his speech, he also made a brief reference to Murphy Brown, a popular TV character played by the accomplished actress Candice Bergen. Murphy Brown, a single, bright, articulate young woman, had gotten pregnant on a weeknight sitcom viewed by a public as enormous as it was credulous. America held its collective breath, waiting for the arrival of the baby! Would it be a boy or a girl? Apparently the illegitimacy of the baby's birth and the problems attached to single parenthood were lost on the American consciousness. The vice president used this media

event as another illustration of the poverty of values afflicting the culture.

Immediately an immense furor developed. Johnny Carson, soon to retire, thanked the V.P. for "coming through" for him again, while David Letterman weighed in with, "Mr. Vice President, I don't know how to tell you this, but Murphy Brown is a fictional character." Feminists of various stripes expressed outrage that the vice president should be so insensitive to the lot of many brave, self-sacrificing single moms, pointing out the inherent nobility of Murphy's action in that she did not abort the child but selflessly went ahead with the confinement and was now embarking on the difficult and often thankless task of raising the child on her own. The talk shows, the call-in shows, the editorial writers, and the politicians, not to mention the preachers, jumped on the bandwagon—and the ratings of Murphy Brown went into the stratosphere. Suddenly the whole issue of values was front and center.

While this was happening, *Newsweek* ran a cover story written by Joe Klein, a senior editor, in which he stated, "Flawed vehicle though he may be, Dan Quayle seems to have nudged presidential politics perilously close to something that really matters: a debate on values and the American family" (8 June 1992, 19).

And so the debate began, and I listened very carefully. But there was something odd about it. As the different sides lined up to state their points of view on values and American society, it was intriguing to me that *all the models referred to were fictional!* So while one side talked earnestly about Murphy Brown, the best their opponents could do was to cite Ozzie and Harriet Nelson. Somewhere along the line, Bart Simpson got into it, and occasionally the values of the African-American middle-class family, the Huxtables, were invoked. If memory serves, we were mercifully spared the Archie Bunkers.

Now, we may find this mildly amusing, but isn't it sad that

in a debate on something as significant and profound as values, the proponents found it necessary to utilize fictional models, created by the media, to make their points? Maybe we are not only suffering from a poverty of values but also a poverty of models. Can't we do better than that?

THE CHURCH IS THE ONLY INSTITUTION THAT IS HOLDING SOME DANGEROUS AREAS OF OUR CITIES TOGETHER.

While the criticisms leveled at the church by people like Nicols Fox do have some validity, in order to be fair, we must give consideration to another side of the issue. The fact is, the church is making a positive impact on communities. In some segments of our society, the church is the only institution having any kind of effect on the subject of values. Recently I was told by a sociologist working in some of the most troubled major cities in America that, in his experience, the church was the only institution that was holding some dangerous areas of the cities together.

So, while it is unlikely that a lot of help will be coming from the educators, the media, or the politicians, perhaps we can be more hopeful about the church. Perhaps God's people can speak out winsomely and compellingly and cast some sweetness and light on the troubled waters of our culture's values. But what exactly does the church have to say on the subject? How well is it being said? And is anybody listening? These are the questions we can explore together in the chapters to come.

TWO

WHOSE VALUES DO YOU VALUE?

I AM writing this chapter in a conference center on the out-skirts of Brasília, the capital city of Brazil. Last evening, after the final session, a group of conferees went down to the snack bar, where one of the veteran missionaries insisted on buying everyone ice cream and a local drink called *guaraná*. He fished an immense bundle of cruzeiros, the Brazilian currency, from his pocket and said with a laugh, "I may as well spend these things because they will have little or no value in the morning."

Brazil is in the grip of roaring inflation, and the currency is losing value at an alarming rate. In a few weeks the government will declare the cruzeiros totally worthless and will issue a new currency. A similar thing happened in Germany many years ago when the reichsmark became valueless and the deutsche mark took its place. I remember a young girl, a member of a party I was leading to Germany many years ago, showing me a fistful of money she had brought to spend on her vacation. When I inquired where she got it, she told me her father had saved it up from the days when he served in the army in Germany. Unfortunately for her, she held in her hand bundles of worthless reichsmarks. They had no value. They could be exchanged for nothing of significance.

Dan Quayle and Meg Greenfield and others were not concerned about the declining worth of cruzeiros and reichsmarks when they talked about values. They had something more significant in mind. The debate over values is more than a discussion of declining currencies, or even economies. What exactly do we mean by *values?*

Discovering What Our Values Are

Hunter Lewis, in *A Question of Values,* defines values as "personal beliefs that propel us to action, to a particular kind of behavior and life."

These beliefs can be held with varying degrees of intensity and thus vary dramatically in the impact they make on behavioral patterns. Hunter Lewis suggests, for instance, that beliefs, in ascending order of intensity, may be demonstrated by *interests, preferences, respect,* and *commitment.* Let me illustrate.

If I work on the age-old premise that "you can always find time to do what you really want to do," then the way I spend my leisure time will be a good indicator of my interests and to a certain extent my values. If I prefer functioning as a "couch potato" rather than training for a marathon, it is a reasonable assumption that I do not highly value physical fitness. Or if I prefer spending leisure time with my grandchildren rather than playing golf, then it would probably be correct to assume that I highly value the extended family. My *interests* help identify my values.

At the risk of raising a hypothetical question that deserves only a hypothetical answer, let me ask you, If you were awakened in the middle of the night by the blare of a fire alarm, and you had minutes to escape the blazing building, what would you grab first? You wouldn't be able to take everything, so you would have to choose between one thing and another. It might require choosing between the cat or the children's photos, the family Bible or the autographed baseball. Which way would you go? What you would choose, all things being equal, would indicate your *preferences* and thus your values.

But we can go further. Ask yourself, *What is it that I treasure so highly that I am irritated when other people don't?* Or to put it another way, *What are the things I respect so deeply that I tend to be resentful of those who treat them with disrespect?* Recently, one of our elderly ushers was incensed when a young man came into church and sat in the pew with a baseball cap on his head—backwards at that! The usher asked me what he should do, and by the look on his face he appeared to be debating whether to take the cap off the head or the head off the shoulders! He was irritated by what appeared to be a total lack of *respect* for something he valued highly. Good, old-time courtesy was high on his list of values, and his irritation for those who did not share his views loudly declared it.

BELIEFS DEEPLY HELD TURN INTO COMMITMENTS FIERCELY DEFENDED.

Beliefs deeply held turn into *commitments* fiercely defended. Taken to their logical conclusion, things worth living for become issues worth dying for. When the Founding Fathers of the United States made their historic decision to sign the Declaration of Independence in 1776, they pledged "our lives, our fortunes and our sacred honor." This was not grandiose rhetoric. They were liable to be charged with treason, and they could have easily lost their livelihoods if not their very lives. But for them the risk had to be taken because what they believed about liberty was significant enough to demand the ultimate commitment. There was no doubt about what they valued.

Burning buildings and revolutions are obviously not the

stuff of normal daily living, but these illustrations serve to identify how we can get in touch with the values we hold. We often go through life barely conscious of them. But identify them we should, and think about them we must.

How Do We Learn Values?

Values are really more than preferences or interests. They are beliefs that produce in us a commitment. And that commitment is so significant that it leads us to behave in a certain way. And our behavior establishes a lifestyle.

Values incorporate a moral component into the people we are and the lives we live. This holds true both at the individual and corporate levels. Values at the personal level determine the type of person we meet on the street; values at the societal level decide the kind of street on which we meet that person. I may meet a mugger or a merchant on the street; that person's values will determine which. The street may be a tree-lined haven where children play contentedly or a burned-out shell of a neighborhood where drug traffickers wage war with automatic weapons; the values of my society and neighborhood will decide which.

But how can lifestyles vary so drastically? How can people believe so differently? How can neighborhoods differ so dramatically?

One reason is that we learn about life differently. Our background, environment, and upbringing have a role in how we come to view life. Hunter Lewis suggests six ways in which we learn values and by which those values are shaped:

- Authority
- Deductive logic
- Sensory experience
- Emotion
- Intuition
- Science

To illustrate how these ways of learning might play out, let's take the situation of a woman discovering she's pregnant.

AUTHORITY. One woman accepts the pope's authority and refuses to have an abortion. Another prefers the government's authority and goes ahead with the abortion since it is legal.

DEDUCTIVE LOGIC. The one argues that killing is wrong, that abortion is killing, and therefore abortion is wrong. But the other argues that the embryo is part of the woman's body, the woman has the right to determine what happens to her own body; therefore, abortion is permissible.

SENSORY EXPERIENCE. One woman will have an abortion because the last time she was pregnant, she felt dreadful. Another woman had a wonderful pregnancy and so will decide to see this one to term.

EMOTION. If a woman has had a traumatic delivery, she may be terrified of facing another and would avert it by abortion. Her neighbor may remember the incredible joy she experienced when her previous baby was born and welcome the pregnancy with delight.

INTUITION. One woman simply intuits that this pregnancy has come at good time, it will be a good experience, and she should go through with it. Another woman may intuit quite the opposite.

SCIENTIFIC STUDY. We are all aware that whenever a scientific study is cited to prove that women who have abortions are susceptible to postabortion guilt feelings, there is always a contradictory "latest" study proving conclusively that the incidence of depression is no greater among women who have abortions than it is for women who suffer postpartum depression.

All these examples simply serve to point out one reason there are so many differing value systems: There are many ways in which we process information, and those ways determine how we come to our personal system of beliefs.

I was raised in a God-fearing family where the Word of God was regarded as the final authority in matters of faith and practice. My parents believed that children should be seen and not heard, should wash their own dishes, clean their own shoes, and not answer back. This early training made it relatively easy for me to accept the rigorous discipline of the Royal Marines in later life. It almost seemed like a relief at times! As a result, I learned to accept authority, and I have never ceased to respect it and learn from it.

But a six-year-old child whose father walks out on the family and takes up with another woman while refusing to pay child support, thus banishing the child and his mother to intense financial and emotional strain, will probably have great difficulty accepting authority and trusting people. He or she would be more likely to learn from bitter emotions and painful experience.

Our learning and believing are affected not only by background but by our assumptions and presuppositions. We normally say, for example, that seeing is believing, when in actual fact the opposite is nearer the truth—believing is seeing. When the disciples *saw* the risen Lord, they *believed* it was a ghost. Why? Because they believed in ghosts but not resurrections! So, all the evidence to the contrary, they believed they saw a ghost, when what they were seeing but not believing was a resurrection. In our lives, as well, we more often respond according to what we *know* than what we haven't yet discovered. And sometimes what we *know* is not quite true or not completely true—or false altogether—while what we have yet to discover could be the very principle that will save us from self-destruction.

Three Possible Foundations for Our Beliefs

Let's say that all of us have received information from a variety of sources via a number of different information highways— our different backgrounds and means of getting knowledge about life. What do we do with the information? There are three very different approaches to this issue, but they have one thing in common: They are all based on presuppositions.

A SIX-YEAR-OLD CHILD WHOSE FATHER WALKS OUT ON THE FAMILY WILL PROBABLY HAVE GREAT DIFFICULTY ACCEPTING AUTHORITY AND TRUSTING PEOPLE.

Self determines what is true and right

This is a common supposition today: Nobody else has the right or the ability to choose for the autonomous self. It is "none of their business." So every person is responsible to come to his or her own conclusions and ignore what everyone else says or thinks about it. Jerry Rubin said that the liberated man "can do what he wants whenever he wants to do it."

That's the self talking, taking charge and calling the shots! Greil Marcus, writing in *Esquire*, said, "I can go where I want, do what I want, say what I want. There are no rules. Freedom's just another word for a mess someone else has to clean up" (August 1992). Apparently the irony of stating "there are no rules" while postulating self-determined rules of freedom bordering on anarchy escaped this liberated gentleman!

W. E. Henley in his famous poem "Invictus" put it less crudely but no less forcefully:

> *In the fell clutch of circumstance,*
> *I have not winced nor cried aloud.*

Under the bludgeonings of chance
my head is bloody, but unbowed.
Beyond this place of wrath and tears
looms but the horror of the shade,
and yet the menace of the years
finds, and shall find, me unafraid.
It matters not how strait the gate,
how charged with punishments the scroll,
I am the master of my fate;
I am the captain of my soul.

Woody Allen, the filmmaker and perennial therapeutic counselee, had a much publicized live-in arrangement with actress Mia Farrow. In the "family" that resulted from this liaison, previous marriages, and numerous adoptions, Woody Allen functioned in a somewhat ambiguous manner as a father figure to the children—until he decided to have an affair with one of the teenage children. Even hard-boiled, scandal-calloused New Yorkers thought this was going too far and said so. Mr. Allen was unhappy with the bad publicity he received, and when challenged by a reporter as to why he would do such a thing, he answered rather truculently, "The heart wants what it wants." This implies, I suppose, that the autonomous self determines what it wants and goes for it without taking anything else into consideration, including the need to explain itself to other people. In other words, the self reigns!

Society decides what is true and right
This is certainly an improvement on the former approach in that at least it acknowledges that the individual cannot go it alone and that society cannot survive when made up of people intent on doing their own thing. Of course, some societies have become so authoritarian that they ignore and even abuse the individuals under their care. A. James Reichley had this in

mind when he insisted, "What democracy needs is a value system that legitimizes both individual rights and social authority and establishes a balance between the two" (Religion in America, The Brookings Institute, 1985, 344).

THERE IS A SOVEREIGN LORD FROM WHOM WE COME, THROUGH WHOM WE LIVE, BY WHOM WE SURVIVE, AND TO WHOM WE ARE ACCOUNTABLE.

But there are still problems when society becomes the determining factor in values. We saw this clearly when the U.S. Supreme Court decided to hear a case dealing with pornography. One of the justices was quite frank about his own dilemma, saying that he had difficulty defining pornography—but he knew it when he saw it. It was hardly surprising when the Court came to the conclusion that pornography is that which offends local community standards. This got them off the hook but impaled just about everybody else. They were going on the assumption that what is pornographic in Peoria is bread and butter in Times Square, and what would make the hair of Bible Belt Baptists stand on end would not even make a hair curl in San Francisco. So much for society deciding values! Obviously this approach raises more questions than it provides answers. Which society? Or, more accurately, which *segment* of society? The majority? The special interest groups? The most vocal? The most powerful? The people with money? The media?

There are those who profess a kind of reverence for the common sense of the American people and their innate ability to know what is right. Politicians are often heard to intone such platitudes when they hope that this infallible populace will be commonsensical enough to vote for them! But Carl Bernstein of Watergate fame is not as impressed:

> We are in the process of creating, in sum, what deserves to be called the idiot culture. Not an idiot sub-culture, which every society has bubbling beneath the surface and which can provide harmless fun, but the culture itself. For the first time in our history the weird and the stupid and the coarse are becoming our cultural norm, even our cultural ideal. (*The Australian*, 13 June 1992)

So, given that society is made up of widely—and wildly—divergent people with special interests, idiosyncrasies, and even idiotic ideals, should we accept that *society* should be the sole determinant of values? I think not!

The sovereign Lord determines what is true and right

Without apology I have saved the best till last. The third possible supposition upon which we can base our value system is this: There is a *sovereign Lord* from whom we come, through whom we live, by whom we survive, and to whom we are accountable. And he is himself the source of all that is of value. It is in his character and his being that those things that are good and right and true are to be found, and he has revealed himself and all his values to us in his Son, Jesus Christ. It is in relationship to this sovereign Lord that we find our system of values. It is through the spiritual life this Son gives us and through the ministry of the Holy Spirit that we can gain insight into these values, as well as obtain the power to put them into practice.

THREE

VALUES, VIRTUES, AND OTHER VOLATILE MATTERS

WE have grown accustomed to thinking in relative terms. Some of us may have tried to work out the answer to this question: How fast is a man traveling as he walks along the corridor of an express train relative *(a)* to a person sitting in the train, *(b)* to a person standing on the platform, and *(c)* to a person walking along the corridor in the opposite direction? We've probably given up and wished we could ask Einstein to explain relativity to us. Legend has it that someone did ask him to do just that, and his reply was, "When a young man sits on a hot stove for a minute, it seems like an hour, but when he meets his girlfriend for an hour, it seems like a minute." I guess that helps, but not much!

There are also some obvious problems when we assume that a "theory of relativity" rules in the realm of our values. Dr. Alasdair MacIntyre of Notre Dame University argues in *After Virtue* that the moral problems we are encountering in modern society can be traced to what he calls "the failure of the Enlightenment project." In a chapter entitled "Why the Enlightenment Project Had to Fail," he explains how classical philosophy assumed three things: "untutored human nature, man-as-he-could-be-if-he-realized-his-*telos,* and the moral precepts which enable him to pass from one state to the other" (University of Notre Dame Press, 1981).

Put into more understandable terms, what thinkers assumed before the Enlightenment was that human nature in its natural state needed help; it needed help to arrive at its potential, and the way of arriving at that potential lay in moral guidelines, i.e., values.

As we can see, the classical thinkers had some major points in common with traditional Christian theology. Christianity claims that people are in a fallen state, that they are meant to live far and above that fallen state, and that getting from "fallen" to our divine potential is ultimately a moral matter. The difference between Christian belief and classical thought, however, is that Christians believe that simply following moral guidelines is not enough; we rely on the forgiveness, grace, and empowering of Christ dwelling within us if we are to ever reach our potential and live beyond the grip of a sinful nature. But the result of Christ in us is quite naturally a change in our morality—a change from a sin-centered life to a God-centered life.

But Dr. MacIntyre notes that during Enlightenment times both theological and classical philosophical thought about humanity were rejected, which served "to eliminate any notion of man-as-he-could-be-if-he-realized-his-*telos*." He goes on to explain:

> Since the whole point of ethics—both as a theoretical and practical discipline—is to enable man to pass from his present state to his true end, the elimination of any notion of essential human nature and with it the abandonment of any notion of *telos* leaves behind a moral scheme composed of two remaining elements whose relationship becomes quite unclear. (*After Virtue*, 54–55)

This is a basic problem. What do we believe about man's "present state" and his "true end"? If we are confused about either, or both, we'll obviously be confused about how to get from one to the other—and this is what values are all about.

> IT IS THE LOSTNESS OF MODERN MAN THAT HAS LED TO THE INEVITABLE CONFUSION ABOUT WHAT HE'S ABOUT AND HOW HE IS TO GET TO WHERE HE'S SUPPOSED TO BE GOING.

The story is told of a young man in a shiny sports car coming to a screeching halt at a crossroads. He shouted to an old countryman who sat outside the pub drinking a glass of ale, "I say, old man, can you tell me the way to London?"

"'Fraid I can't, young fella," he replied.

"Well, how far is it to St. Albans?"

"Couldn't tell you that for sure, either."

"You don't know much, do you?" the young man said in exasperation.

"You're right there, young fella. But I'm not lost."

It is the lostness of modern man, who has dispensed with any sense of who he is or where he's going, that has led to the inevitable confusion about what he's about and how he is to get to where he's supposed to be going. This is the essence of our confusion about values. Yogi Berra was right when he said, "If you don't know where you're going, you may end up someplace else." It is the wide variety of "someplace(s) else" at which people are arriving—because of no definitive sense of where they are going—that accounts for the relativistic confusion in which so many people today are floundering.

Are We Talking about Values or Virtue?

Some people who have joined the debate about values want to avoid the actual word *values.* They prefer to use *virtue* as did Dr. MacIntyre in the title of the book I've been quoting. But this word carries some unnecessary baggage that doesn't always further the discussion. As Kenneth L. Woodward wrote in a cover article in *Newsweek:* "Virtue: For too many Americans, the word suggests only a bygone era, prim lectures on sexual purity—at best, something you 'lose' when you finally give in or give up" (13 June 1994, 38).

But why do people dislike *values* and gravitate toward *virtue?* Woodward goes on to explain:

> Values is a morally neutral term that merely indicates preference and can be quite banal. . . . A virtue, by contrast, is a quality of character by which individuals habitually recognize and *do* the right thing.

In today's debate, most people would mean by values what other people mean by virtues without necessarily thinking of concepts from a "bygone era." Society in general has dismissed the "bygones," which for many people means they should "be gone."

But let's give the "bygones" their due. Their concept of virtue initially included such qualities as "prudence, justice, fortitude and temperance" (Woodward, 38). But as MacIntyre explained, Aristotle, who taught the above four virtues, was followed by later generations who added others such as loyalty and obedience, before the Christians weighed in with faith, hope, and love. Even later suggestions were made that humility (which the Greeks despised) and compassion should be added to the list. Do we really want these bygone virtues to be gone?

Newsweek, somewhat unkindly, has given the name *Virtuecrats* to those who are trying to introduce these concepts into the public arena because their approach is in danger of politicizing the process, which could give the whole project the kiss of death. Politics aside, there is a major flaw in what Woodward describes as the Virtuecrats' position. They assume that virtuous people "habitually recognize and *do* the right thing" (his italics). This kind of thinking leaves little room for the historical biblical doctrine of human fallenness and will naturally lead to unrealistic expectations of what humans can do through a system of virtues alone.

For this reason, I will stay with the term *values,* as much as it has been overused and misunderstood. But in referring to values I do not assume, as many do, that it is a morally neutral term. What few people realize is that values are really the modern equivalent of an ancient Old Testament concept. What concept might that be? Goodness? Righteousness? Holiness?

> *The Lord brought me forth as the first of his works,*
> *before his deeds of old;*
> *I was appointed from eternity,*
> *from the beginning, before the world began.*
> Proverbs 8:22-23

The speaker in this passage is Wisdom, who is often our narrator in Proverbs, the ancient Bible book of wise sayings. While we can talk about getting our values from the self or from society, this passage points to an awesome concept: *The fundamental values of life are to be found in the character of God that existed before the worlds were made.*

Start at the Beginning: Wisdom

The word *wisdom* has interesting connections and connotations. The old craftsmen who worked long and hard on the intricate furnishings of the tabernacle according to the instructions given by the Lord to Moses were recognized as having received special "skill" from the Lord (Exod. 31:6). In Psalm 107 the psalmist graphically portrays the terror of sailors caught in a storm where they are "at their wits' end" (Ps. 107:27). And in 1 Kings 3:9 we are told about the humble request of Solomon, who, realizing the immensity of the task God had given him, asked that he might be given "a discerning heart . . . to distinguish between right and wrong." In each of these examples the word used to describe the special skills of craftsmen, sailors, and king is closely related to the word for wisdom. In its original usage the word simply meant "skill," but with the passage of time it broadened to mean "skill in living." So William E. Mouser Jr. defines *wisdom* in *Walking in Wisdom*: "The practical skills to live successfully and the moral discipline to learn and implement those skills" (InterVarsity Press, 1983, 20).

In the Hebrew community, with its unique relationship to God, skillful living was synonymous with keeping the moral standards of the covenant as outlined by the Lord. So Allen P. Ross writes in *Expositor's Bible Commentary*:

> In the book of Proverbs "wisdom" signifies skillful living—the ability to make wise choices and live successfully according to the moral standards of the covenant community. The one who lives skillfully produces things of lasting value to God and the community." (vol. 5, Zondervan, 1991, 905)

What we see, then, is that wisdom as understood in the ancient writings of the people of God amounted to an understanding of the principles handed down by the Lord to his people in order that they might live wisely and well. Undoubtedly this kind of living would be beneficial for the individual and for society, but more than that it would conform to the *telos* for which human beings were created, redeemed, and called into fellowship with the Creator. In other words, we could call wisdom the ancient system of values handed down to us by God so that we could live, governed not by self-determined standards or even by societally approved standards, but by the sovereign Lord's divinely ordained standards—which would prove in the long run to be in the best interests of both the individual and society. So let us look further into the Old Testament idea of wisdom. And what better place to start than the section called the "wisdom literature" and, specifically, the book of Proverbs.

THE FUNDAMENTAL VALUES OF LIFE ARE TO BE FOUND IN THE CHARACTER OF GOD THAT EXISTED BEFORE THE WORLDS WERE MADE.

Most cultures include proverbs in their heritage. They are a collection of tested and true maxims preserved for the good of succeeding generations. Usually they are pithy and pointed sayings designed to catch the attention and stick in the memory. All of us have, cataloged in our minds, such sayings as A stitch in time saves nine, or To be forewarned is to be forearmed. But while the Old Testament book contains all the above characteristics, it is unique in that it is part of God's inspired Word and therefore deserves special attention.

The introduction to the book of Proverbs states its purpose clearly:

> *The proverbs of Solomon son of David, king of Israel:*
> *for attaining wisdom and discipline;*
> *for understanding words of insight;*
> *for acquiring a disciplined and prudent life,*
> *doing what is right and just and fair;*
> *for giving prudence to the simple,*
> *knowledge and discretion to the young—*
> *let the wise listen and add to their learning,*
> *and let the discerning get guidance—*
> *for understanding proverbs and parables,*
> *the sayings and riddles of the wise.*
> *The fear of the Lord is the beginning of knowledge,*
> *but fools despise wisdom and discipline.* Proverbs 1:1-7

Meanings of Wisdom

Clustered around the word *wisdom* in this introductory statement are many other words that help us develop what is meant by wisdom and that also describe what we now call values—or, if you prefer, virtues. "Discipline," "understanding," "insight," "prudence," "right, and just and fair" all turn up in this introduction of the wisdom book.

Discipline

Wisdom includes discipline, which in this context means instruction and training involving correction and development of moral character. Proverbs is full of references to discipline, but we need only look at a few to understand its basic meanings and implications for living. Consider the following:

> *My son, do not despise the Lord's discipline*
> *and do not resent his rebuke.* Proverbs 3:11

The evil deeds of a wicked man ensnare him;
the cords of his sin hold him fast.
He will die for lack of discipline,
led astray by his own great folly. 5:22-23

The corrections of discipline are the way to life. 6:23b

Whoever loves discipline loves knowledge,
but he who hates correction is stupid. 12:1

He who spares the rod hates his son,
but he who loves him is careful to discipline him. 13:24

A fool spurns his father's discipline,
but whoever heeds correction shows prudence. 15:5

Folly is bound up in the heart of a child,
but the rod of discipline will drive it far from him. 22:15

Buy the truth and do not sell it;
get wisdom, discipline and understanding. 23:23

Discipline your son, and he will give you peace;
he will bring delight to your soul. 29:17

While much of the emphasis in these proverbs is on the disciplining of young people, we know that discipline is for all ages. And, even though it is unpleasant at times, discipline is vitally necessary for the development of a lifestyle that pleases God and brings blessing to all concerned. Tom Landry, the legendary former coach of the Dallas Cowboys and a committed believer, speaking of discipline as it relates to professional athletics, said, "The job of a coach is to make men do what they don't want to do, in order to be what they've always wanted to be."

He was referring to the fact that some athletes think their natural talents are so great that they do not need to practice, stay in shape, or work out with the team. But if they want to be the superstars they think they are, they will have to do the things that they, in their own warped understanding, regard as unnecessary and unpleasant.

His comments can be applied to any person, athlete or otherwise, who not only takes seriously the business of being what he or she has "always wanted to be" but, more important, who seeks to be "all God intended" him or her to be. Discipline—that is, the instruction, training and correction, and development of moral character—must be a major part of a value system.

Understanding

The same can be said for "understanding." There are many references to understanding in the Old Testament, but a few quotes from Proverbs will suffice:

> *For the Lord gives wisdom,*
> *and from his mouth come knowledge and understanding.*
> Proverbs 2:6

> *Discretion will protect you,*
> *and understanding will guard you.* 2:11

> *By wisdom the Lord laid the earth's foundations,*
> *by understanding he set the heavens in place.* 3:19

> *Wisdom is supreme; therefore get wisdom.*
> *Though it cost all you have, get understanding.* 4:7

> *You who are simple, gain prudence;*
> *you who are foolish, gain understanding.* 8:5

> *The fear of the Lord is the beginning of wisdom,*
> *and knowledge of the Holy One is understanding.* 9:10

> *A fool finds pleasure in evil conduct,*
> *but a man of understanding delights in wisdom.* 10:23

A man who lacks judgment derides his neighbor,
but a man of understanding holds his tongue. 11:12

He who ignores discipline despises himself,
but whoever heeds correction gains understanding. 15:32

How much better to get wisdom than gold,
to choose understanding rather than silver! 16:16

Understanding is a fountain of life to those who have it,
but folly brings punishment to fools. 16:22

A man of knowledge uses words with restraint,
and a man of understanding is even-tempered. 17:27

A fool finds no pleasure in understanding
but delights in airing his own opinions. 18:2

A man who strays from the path of understanding
comes to rest in the company of the dead. 21:16

Buy the truth and do not sell it;
get wisdom, discipline and understanding. 23:23

By wisdom a house is built,
and through understanding it is established. 24:3

Hebrew poetry sometimes uses parallelism, which at times means that terms like *wisdom* and *understanding* are almost synonymous. Even so, it's clear that *understanding* has a special meaning which is perhaps best illustrated in 1 Kings 3:9 where it describes Solomon's ability to distinguish between right and wrong. *To gain understanding* in this sense means to have the God-given capacity to "discern between." It is worth noting that the old-fashioned virtue called prudence has been defined as "the ability to make the right choice in specific situations" (*Newsweek*, 13 June 1994, 38). So whether we talk about the ability to "discern between" or "the ability to make the right choice," it is obvious that "understanding" in Proverbs or "prudence" according to Aristotle and his friends requires a sense of what is different. And it includes the ability to discriminate between options, using some objective standard of evaluation.

King Solomon once had to discern between the rival claims of two women to one baby. Only one of the women could be the mother, and only the mother had a just claim to the baby. It is a famous story: Solomon decided that he should just divide the child in half with a sword so that each woman could have her share, knowing, of course, that the real mother would love her child so much that she would give it up to the other woman rather than see it killed. So by means of this risky challenge, Solomon identified the true mother, distinguished between the competing claims, discriminated against the one, discerned the true nature of the other, and made his decision. That's *understanding.* Most of us will never be called upon to make this serious a judgment—although the people who work in our domestic court systems have to make similar judgments all the time. But all of us do have to make choices between right and wrong. Wisdom and understanding enable us to make good judgments.

On a recent TV talk show called *Sonya Live,* directed and hosted by Dr. Sonya Friedman on CNN, there was an interesting conversation between Dr. Friedman and another psychologist, during which the guest made this telling statement: "When we were young our most prized possession was our virginity. My daughter's generation can't wait to give it away. I guess values change!" I was particularly struck by the sense of dismay and regret projected by these two cultured women as they discussed changing values—without in any way grappling with the rightness or wrongness of the competing values or our need to discern between them.

It seems that choosing between one course of action and

another, on the basis of any moral qualification, is something that most people are simply not willing to do. And in relinquishing their right to discern and discriminate, they are letting go of understanding and thus losing their grip on a solid value system.

CHOOSING BETWEEN COURSES OF ACTION ON THE BASIS OF ANY MORAL QUALIFICATION IS SOMETHING THAT MOST PEOPLE ARE SIMPLY NOT WILLING TO DO.

Prudence

The *prudent life* is described as "doing what is right and just and fair."

It is interesting that this understanding of prudence is also very close to the classical virtues of justice and temperance. The former is defined as "fairness, honesty, lawfulness and the ability to keep one's promises" and the latter as "self-discipline, the control of unruly human passions and appetites" (Woodward, *Newsweek*, 13 June 1994, 38–39).

Doing what was right in the book of Proverbs meant adhering to correct standards. There is a clear example of this in the way that the children of Israel were told, "Do not have two differing measures in your house—one large, one small. You must have accurate and honest weights and measures" (Deut. 25:14-15).

I can still remember the feelings of apprehension I experienced as a boy when the Weights and Measures inspector arrived periodically, unannounced, at my father's store and checked the weights and measures to see if they were accurate according to government standards. My father did not share my apprehension because he was as honest as the day is long. Nevertheless, we were required to get the weights and measures right, and if through the process of normal wear and tear the weights had become inaccurate or the measures had been dented, adjustments had to be made.

The laws as presented in Deuteronomy (and various other places in the Old Testament) likewise did not allow any changing of the weights. Measurements remained constant, no matter who was selling and who was buying. And if we carry this principle further, we have the sense that what is right, is right; what is fair, is fair; and these values do not change.

The attitude that says, "I can do whatever I like in the privacy of my own home, and it is irrelevant to my standing in public," did not wash in those days, and it should not in ours. The naive assumption that what a politician does in his private life is irrelevant to his or her capacity to function well in public life had no place in biblical thinking. They were closer to believing that "what a man is in the dark on his own is what a man really is." One set of standards ruled at home and in business.

Prudence not only dictated that actions should be right but also that they should be just. While there is an obvious connection between the two, a just action requires that decisions relating to it be appropriate to the situation, as we convey in the statement "Let the punishment fit the crime." We need not limit the idea of justice in Proverbs to this meaning; justice must come to bear on situations outside our judicial/legal system. But our present judicial system provides a good illustration of this concept.

U.S. News and World Report (1 November 1982) reported that for every thousand index crimes committed, only five hundred are reported. Of the five hundred crimes reported, arrests are made in only one hundred of them—and four hundred go unsolved. Of the one hundred people who are arrested, thirty-five are referred to juvenile court, where thirty of them have their cases dismissed and five go to jail. Of the sixty-five referred to adult court, twenty-five are rejected by the prosecutor, six jump bail or have their case dismissed, two are acquitted, twelve are put on probation, and the remainder go to jail. According to my reckoning, that means that out of one thousand index crimes—in layman's terms that means "big ones"—five juveniles and twenty adults go to jail. That works out at 2.5 percent! Then bear in mind that because most jails are overcrowded, some judges are ordering the release of nonviolent criminals, and so most of the 2.5 percent probably will not serve their full sentences. So the question is, assuming that the law of the land is just and that criminals who commit index crimes should (rightly or wrongly) go to jail, is justice being done when less than 2.5 percent of them ever serve an appropriate sentence? The answer is pretty obvious.

Many reasons are given for this breakdown of justice and this emergency situation where crime is concerned—and many remedies are offered by those on all sides of the issue. I use it merely as an illustration of the fact that the concept of "fair and just" is no longer so well defined in our culture.

Fairness

Every little child has concepts of fairness. Every parent at some time or other has been alarmed to hear bloodcurdling screams from one of their progeny only to discover, on arriving out of breath at the scene of the crime, that junior is screaming blue murder because his sibling has got the last green candy that he wanted and "it's not fair." Where these precious little ones derive their idea of fairness I will leave to the developmental psychologists to discover, but I do know that for little people *fair* usually means, "I have lost the advantage which by right belongs to me!"

This, of course, is not what Proverbs meant by *fair*, although youngsters certainly aren't the only ones who operate by this definition! The real meaning of *fair* is "to behave uprightly."

Upright is a word that makes people nervous, maybe because it is too close to *uptight*. But there's no more connection between upright and uptight than between *meekness* and *weakness*—although these latter words are also often combined and confused. The upright are those who believe that what God says is right, seek to do what he says, and thus live rightly. Because we live in community rather than in isolation, this usually includes treating people rightly. To be fair, or to live uprightly, therefore, has vertical connections with the divine and horizontal connections with other people.

What Does It Mean to Be Foolish?

What is your definition of a fool? Is it a stupid person? a class clown? someone who doesn't take life seriously? Let's take a look at a very serious definition. Blaise Pascal, the brilliant French mathematician and philosopher, wrote in his famous *Pensées:*

> There are only three kinds of persons; those who serve God having found Him; others who are occupied in seeking Him, not having found Him; while the remainder live without seeking Him and without having found Him. The first are reasonable and happy, the last are foolish and unhappy; those between are unhappy and reasonable. (IV:257, 220)

By Pascal's definition, a foolish person was one who was living without seeking God and, consequently, not finding him. This is the essence of foolishness in Proverbs.

The way of a fool seems right to him,
but a wise man listens to advice. Proverbs 12:15

He who walks with the wise grows wise,
but a companion of fools suffers harm. 13:20

A wise man fears the Lord and shuns evil, but a
fool is hotheaded and reckless. 14:16

A fool finds no pleasure in understanding
but delights in airing his own opinions. 18:2

There once was a woman who was married to a man who didn't deserve her. So what's new? But in this case he was extra bad, and she was quite extraordinarily special. He was a fool in the biblical sense of the word. That does not mean he was stupid, dumb, or given to zany humor. It means that he despised wisdom—he was opposed to all that we have been talking about and in a surly and mean-spirited way.

His name was Nabal, which, incidentally, means "fool" in the Hebrew. (His mother must have been no fool to recognize one so early!) He got himself into deep trouble with soon-to-be-king David, who was in no mood to be messed with. And if it had not been for Nabal's wife, Abigail, whom we are told was "intelligent and beautiful," he would have been summarily dealt with by His Irate Majesty and his men. As it happened, Abigail demonstrated wisdom, discipline, understanding, and prudence by intercepting the king, making amends, averting disaster, and generally illustrating wisdom in the fullest sense of the word. When her husband found out how close to death he had been because of his own behavior, he promptly had a massive coronary and died anyway. David, meanwhile, comforted the grieving widow (who apparently wasn't too distraught that "the old fool" had passed on), married her, and she lived happily ever after.

Great story? Yes. But great wisdom, or great values, added up to a great woman. And David was a lucky man to find such a treasure.

But now that we have explored some of the meanings of wisdom and have seen how it relates to our modern understanding of values, we need to press on to find out where this wisdom—these values—are to be found and how they can be nurtured and nourished in daily life.

FOUR

THE BEST PLACE TO BEGIN IS THE BEGINNING

ONE of my numerous grandsons, Drew Golz, went to his first baseball game when he was about two and a half years old. He sat with his father in the crowd at Wrigley Field in Chicago and watched the Chicago Cubs go through their annual disappearing act. But he enjoyed the experience and talked to me on the phone about it.

"What did you see, Drew?" I asked him.

"One, two, three, four, five, touchdown!" he replied with great enthusiasm.

I wasn't sure if he was confused about the game he had been watching, or if the reason for the Cubs' lack of success was that they were confused about which game they were playing! But my daughter, Drew's mother, came on the phone and clarified the situation. "He's confused, Dad. He saw the numbers on the scoreboard, and because he's learning his numbers and his alphabet and baseball and football all at the same time, he's a little mixed up!"

Well, being an Englishman, I fully understand the necessity of learning my alphabet and numbers—if not baseball and American football—because all of us, however accomplished, must begin with basics. Shakespeare began with his alphabet, Einstein with his numbers.

1, 2, 3, 4, 5, with or without a touchdown.

A, B, C, D, E, F, with or without a home run.

In all walks of life we must start at the beginning and begin with the basics. So let's talk about the basics of values. The 1, 2, 3s and the ABCs of wisdom. Immediately we are in for a surprise.

The Fear of the Lord

The introduction to Proverbs ends with 1:7:

> *The fear of the Lord is the beginning of knowledge,*
> *but fools despise wisdom and discipline.*

The same thought is expressed slightly differently in Proverbs 9:10:

> *The fear of the Lord is the beginning of wisdom,*
> *and knowledge of the Holy One is understanding.*

Although, as we have seen, "knowledge," "discipline," and "understanding" have different connotations, they are often used interchangeably. But in these and many other powerful statements in Proverbs it is the "fear of the Lord" that is the basis, the foundation, the starting point of wisdom or a system of values.

Now, if the fear of the Lord is so important, we need to know what it means. Recently when I quoted a verse that included the phrase *the fear of the Lord,* someone came to me after the talk and said, "I was brought up in a religious system where we were basically trained to be scared of God. I spent all my years as a kid feeling guilty because I'd been doing stuff I shouldn't have done, waiting for the heavens to drop in on my head and for God to zap me. In the end I just threw it all over. I figured if he was going to get me, he would get me, and there was nothing I could do about it. So for twenty-five years I just did what I wanted and figured when God was good and ready he'd get me. But then one day I found your church, where you weren't into that kind of stuff, and I discovered God loved me unconditionally. Everything changed. I knew I was loved. Forgiven. It was so free, so friendly and fun, and now you're trying to put 'the fear of God' into us again! I don't need this stuff. I'm out of here!"

IF GOD WERE MEAN AND UNFORGIVING, THEN WE WOULD BE RIGHT TO FEAR HIM IN THE WAY WE WOULD FEAR AN ABUSIVE PARENT OR AN OPPRESSIVE GOVERNMENT.

What the fear of the Lord isn't

This is a fairly common experience, and we should begin by explaining what the fear of the Lord is *not*. If God were mean and vindictive and unforgiving, then we would be right to fear him in the way we would fear an abusive parent or an oppressive government. The fact is, Scripture emphasizes through both testaments the loving-kindness and mercy of God. Jesus Christ demonstrated God's attitude toward us as he reached out to heal us, forgive us, and answer our questions. He proved to us that God is approachable, that the Holy God actually wants to be in relationship with us. However, any relationship requires that each party recognize the identity of the other party. The "fear of the Lord" then, is an *attitude* toward God that relates rightly to who he is. And we can only relate rightly to who God is if we understand who he is.

My good friend Phil Hacking, a well-known Anglican minister, and his wife were hiking in the English countryside. They came to a place where the farmer had built a fence across a public pathway. Phil's wife said to him, "There's the farmer up on the hill—let's go and tell him that he has no right putting a fence across a public path." So they climbed the hill to where the farmer and his man were working and confronted him. He stopped his work and listened politely to their indignant expostulations. While Phil was expressing his righteous indignation, however, he was puzzled to see that his wife, who had insisted he should complain, was making faces at him behind the farmer's back, telling him to stop. He ignored her, said his piece, the farmer promised to rectify the error, and they went on their way.

"Didn't you recognize him?" asked his wife.

"No," replied Phil, "he was just the farmer, and he needed to be told."

"You idiot!" she replied. "That was Prince Charles. The Prince of Wales!"

"Well," said Phil, surprised and abashed but undaunted, "it doesn't matter who he is. He shouldn't have built the fence where he did."

"I agree," she answered, "but you could have shown a little more respect!"

"You're right," Phil admitted. "If I'd known who he was, I'd have shown a little more respect."

Now, that's the point. If we knew who God really is we'd show him a little more respect. The problem in the modern world is that too often there is an inadequate knowledge of God. There's a lot of speculation as to who God is and what he's like. But we need to operate on the basis of revelation, not speculation. It is one thing for us to express what we think God is like; it is an entirely different thing for us to recognize what God says he is like. I often hear people say, "Oh, I don't believe God would ever do *that!*" This despite the fact that he has said he will do precisely *that!* Speculation at the expense of revelation leads only to confusion.

What better place to discover who God is than in his self-description when talking to Moses on Mount Sinai: "The compassionate and gracious God, slow to anger, abounding in love and faithfulness, maintaining love to thousands, and forgiving wickedness, rebellion and sin" (Exod. 34:6-7).

Isn't that wonderful? Isn't it exciting to know that God is compassionate and gracious and forgiving and slow to anger and faithful and loving and kind? But that's only part of the picture. For he went on to say, "Yet he does not leave the guilty unpunished; he punishes the children and their children for the sin of the fathers to the third and fourth generation" (Exod. 34:7).

We must make sure that we have a well-rounded picture of who God is. God is fundamentally holy, good, just, right, and fair, which means that if we contravene his laws, if we insult who he is, resist his guidance, and ignore his direction, he must respond in a manner that is in keeping with his holy, just, right, and fair character. He must, if he is true to himself, deal with us in righteous judgment. Truly it is "a dreadful thing to fall into the hands of the living God" (Heb. 10:31).

But if we will admit that we were wrong and repent of what we have done, we will find that he will overwhelm us with his grace and loving-kindness and forgiveness. In fact, our grasp of God's love and grace is directly related to our understanding of his righteousness and holiness. And our appreciation of his forgiveness is in direct proportion to our knowledge of his judgment.

All this comes together in the Cross of our Lord Jesus, which shows God the Father's intense distaste for our rebellion and sin and demonstrates his intense desire to forgive us. Do you want a vision of divine wrath? of intense holiness? of righteous judgment? Look at the Cross! Do you want to know divine love? mercy? grace? Look at the Cross. But don't look at either dimension of the divine character in isolation. Don't try to grasp grace without seeing judgment. Don't expect to appreciate God's mercy without being stunned by his holiness.

What then is the fear of the Lord?
I suggest that it is an attitude toward God that shrinks back in fear before experiencing forgiveness and draws close in awe when forgiven. The unforgiven sinner overwhelmed with feelings of shame before a holy God rightly draws back in fear until she hears the invitation to draw near, which she does with a compelling sense of awe. There is no contradiction here. Alpine climbers revel in the thrill of scaling the majestic heights but must never lose sight of the awesomeness of the mountain. Deep-sea fishermen toil with joy and garner a harvest in the foaming waves, but they know they must never treat the mighty rolling ocean with anything but respect. Small aircraft pilots, they tell me, come in two varieties: old ones and bold ones. There are no old, bold ones. Those who enjoy the freedom of flying like a bird do so conscious of the awesomeness of the heavens in which they soar.

The fear of the Lord involves glad submission to his gracious majesty. Notice that submission is defined by gladness, and his majesty is seen to be gracious. Our overriding desire, therefore, is to honor his majesty and respect his authority while appropriating his grace, reveling in his love, basking in his forgiveness, and seeking only to please him. And our deepest concern is that we do not besmirch his glory or dishonor his name. This is what it means to fear the Lord, and this understanding is fundamental to our system of values.

Some people have expressed concern that I am majoring on

Old Testament concepts that are no longer relevant in these days of grace. Is it so important to think about the fear of the Lord anymore? Didn't Jesus describe God as a loving Father, and doesn't the first letter of John tell us that perfect love casts out fear? Aren't we finished with this God of judgment? Not if we note the New Testament's references to this healthy, holy fear. For example, one of the main criticisms that God levels at the human race is precisely, "there is no fear of God before their eyes" (Rom. 3:18).

> JESUS CHRIST DEMONSTRATED GOD'S ATTITUDE TOWARD US AS HE REACHED OUT TO HEAL US, FORGIVE US, AND ANSWER OUR QUESTIONS.

Moreover, one of the greatest motivational statements of the New Testament is, "Let us purify ourselves from everything that contaminates body and spirit, perfecting holiness out of reverence for God [or fear of the Lord]" (2 Cor. 7:1).

It is worth noting the description of the early church given in Acts 9. This was a church that had greatly feared the persecution of Saul of Tarsus. After Saul became converted the church entered a time of peace and thanksgiving. The Scriptures say in verse 31 that they were strengthened, encouraged in the Spirit, and they grew numerically. But all this happened as they were "living in the fear of the Lord." They were evangelistic. They were worshipful. They had tremendous fellowship. They had a great time together. And they were multiplying dramatically. It was apparently what some people today would call "a fun church to be part of." But fun or not, this remarkable church operated under the umbrella of acknowledging the Lord, being conscious of his awesome majesty and the necessity for their glad submission to him. They lived in the fear of the Lord.

So let's accept the legitimacy of developing a keen fear of the Lord today also, without in any sense losing sight of the wonders of grace and the thrills of forgiveness and fellowship with him. And let's look further into how we can develop this attitude in ourselves.

How Do We Come to a Fear of the Lord?

Wisdom does not grow on trees; neither does the fear of the Lord just happen. There are steps to be taken, as outlined in Proverbs:

> *My son, if you accept my words*
> *and store up my commands within you,*
> *turning your ear to wisdom*
> *and applying your heart to understanding,*
> *and if you call out for insight*
> *and cry aloud for understanding,*
> *and if you look for it as for silver*
> *and search for it as for hidden treasure,*
> *then you will understand the fear of the Lord,*
> *and find the knowledge of God.* Proverbs 2:1-5

In other words, wisdom is the result of not only desire but active seeking. If we acknowledge that fools despise wisdom, we also acknowledge that all of us have to come to the point of deciding whether or not we want to be bothered with what God says. There's a Nabal in all of us. There's a heart that is resistant and a will that is rebellious.

Sometimes it takes a mammoth step for us to start looking at things God's way after a lifetime of doing it our own way. For many people it takes a monumental crisis for them to begin to look at where society's values have taken them and likewise to take a hard look at what God has said. A friend of mine who had lived a number of years in a rebellious, independently minded attitude said that it was only when he "became sick and tired of being sick and tired" that he returned to the principles he had learned in his childhood and rejected in his adolescence.

There is no shortage of discouraged, disillusioned people who have felt let down by their lives. Marvin Hamlisch was the toast of Los Angeles the night in April 1974 when he won three Oscars at the Academy Awards. But he said, "Three Oscars in my hands, and I come home and empty the cat litter. I had thought that success would make me happy but it didn't" (*People*, 10 Dec. 1992, 89).

Shortly after his late-night TV show, watched by millions, was rated second only to Johnny Carson, Arsenio Hall said, "I guess we're a success, but it doesn't feel like I thought it would" (*TV Guide*, 30 Sept. 1989, 18).

We don't have to look far to find illustrations of lives filled with the emptiness of self-gratification. Not a few people from all walks of life arrive at this point of dismay and finally, almost as a last resort, begin to consider God. But at least they begin to explore his truth. They are open to mining for wisdom.

But not everybody who begins to question their value system and its failure to come through for them is willing to explore the truth of God with the tenacity and expectancy of a silver miner. While they are unhappy with the way things are, they suspect that they might be unhappier if they made changes in God's direction. To surrender the "self" approach to values and to adopt the submissive approach to God's way means giving up the autonomy that, although it has failed to satisfy, is still cherished as possibly a person's greatest treasure. And in rejecting society's version of what is "normal," a person opens himself to charges by friends and relatives of "not living in the real world."

There are also those who are open to a quick-fix religious experience without necessarily being willing to turn their ear to wisdom and applying their heart to understanding. In such cases the quick fix becomes only quick and ineffective.

How Does a Fear of the Lord Affect My Behavior?

But let's assume that you are open to exploring God's system of values. Practically speaking, how do we behave if our lives operate out of a system of values that is based on the fear of the Lord?

Hate evil.

> *To fear the Lord is to hate evil.* Proverbs 8:13

I believe everybody on God's green earth finds something utterly distasteful and despicable—something they classify as evil. I don't believe there is anyone so totally reprobate that they cannot condemn at least one thing as out-and-out evil. Oskar Schindler, whose story was immortalized in Steven Spielberg's movie, *Schindler's List,* was a renowned drunkard and womanizer who treated his wife, Emilie, dreadfully but risked his life and lost his fortune countering the evil he saw in the Nazis. Even primitive tribes that we consider barbaric have their codes of admirable and abhorrent behavior. Everybody knows evil in some form or other and hates it. But the trouble is that everybody has their own special hatred for a specific kind of evil while simultaneously cherishing a secret love for their own favorite evil. To hate evil does not mean to hate it selectively, but to be open to seeing evil in all its manifestations and from the divine perspective. To be willing to see some things that I cherish as evil by God's reckoning. To become angry about the things I casually tolerate but which God abhors.

Years ago in our youth work in England we had a young boy called Kenny whose main gift appeared to be breaking windows. Nothing we said or did managed to persuade him that there was something fundamentally wrong about his approach to glass in frames. Until we put him in charge of the windows. Then his perspective changed by 180 degrees. He saw things through the eyes of leadership, and his behavior was transformed. He was on the inside looking out instead of being on the outside breaking in. And with the change of heart came a dramatic alteration in his value system!

But there's another problem we all face when it comes to confronting evil. Have you ever been caught enjoying a good

---

DON'T TRY TO GRASP GRACE WITHOUT SEEING JUDGMENT. DON'T EXPECT TO APPRECIATE GOD'S MERCY WITHOUT BEING STUNNED BY HIS HOLINESS.

---

meal in front of the television when suddenly you discovered you were viewing pictures of a famine? Did you lose your appetite or change the channel? Do you ever watch movies that portray the most incredible violence and thoroughly enjoy it because the bad guys "got theirs"? And did your input of violence on TV ever leave you unmoved when you saw news pictures of real people being blown away? You know what was happening, don't you? You were being desensitized by familiarity with evil. The fact that around the world people are actually being blown away was no longer a concern.

Now, if it is possible for us to be desensitized to things simply because we've become used to them, and we are unable or unwilling to evaluate what is happening to us, then the desensitizing, eroding effect of our culture will do its work unhindered. What if we have nothing to show us that evil is evil and wrong is wrong? We get so used to people calling wrong right and evil good that we lose track of our bearings. We may find ourselves doing evil without knowing it or, worse, without even worrying about it.

But there's one safety net. The fear of the Lord will sensitize us to evil. When we read regularly in God's Word about the activities and attitudes God hates, we won't take them for granted so easily in our daily lives. Read what Jesus said about hypocrisy; read what the prophet Amos said about injustice and oppression of the poor; read what Paul said about the devastating effects of sexual immorality. All of these are serious issues to a holy God, who explains his displeasure with them very specifically. And as we adopt God's view—God's values—we will discover that our hearts and minds begin to experience pain and horror when we see or hear evil. We will begin to hate what the Lord hates, and this will help us keep our values in place.

Fear the right thing.

> He who fears the Lord has a secure fortress.
> Proverbs 14:26

Franklin D. Roosevelt once told the people of the United States, "We have nothing to fear but fear itself." That was probably great presidential rhetoric and was possibly a very helpful thing to say to a discouraged nation, but it was incorrect. To tell people that there's nothing to fear but fear itself is to ignore the one fear that is necessary: the fear of the Lord. Then we can say with assurance, "Fear the Lord and you have nothing else to fear." Why? Because the fear of the Lord is a secure fortress.

Rupert Brooks was a poet who knew firsthand the ghastly, inhumane conditions of the trenches in the First World War, in which he eventually met an untimely death. He wrote in "Safety":

> *Safe shall be my going.*
> *Secretly armed against all death's endeavour;*
> *Safe though all safety's lost; safe where men fall;*
> *And if these poor limbs die, safest of all.*

Feelings of insecurity lead to all kinds of behavioral excesses and relational problems. I have met a number of men who are totally threatened by being married to sharp women who earn more than they do. Their inability to cope has produced deep anger that at times has burst out in verbal and eventual physical abuse. These men, impoverished in their own manhood through their lack of security as persons, take the only course in which they feel superior—physical domination of the female. The fear of the Lord would go a long way in dealing with such unacceptable behavior. First of all, because the man would recognize that he will answer to an awesome Lord for his abusive treatment of divine creation. Second, in reverencing the Lord, a man would discover that the Lord made him uniquely special in his own right, and he has no need to compete where he cannot and no cause to compare where he comes out on the short end of the comparison.

Look for safety.

> *The fear of the Lord is a fountain of life,*
> *turning a man from the snares of death.*   Proverbs 14:27

I was thinking recently that the old-fashioned, rigid rules of my fundamentalist heritage, which I was less than enthusiastic about as I grew up, nevertheless delivered me from a lot of things that could be called, at the risk of seeming overly dramatic, "the snares of death." The three golden rules were no smoking, no drinking, and no sex before marriage. As I embarked on my business career and later served in the Royal Marines, I quickly discovered that I was in a tiny minority as far as these rules were concerned. It was not easy. I spent a lot of time living in close quarters with people who not only regarded my behavior as odd but openly questioned whether I didn't have some problems that they thought were their duty to solve! But years later I sometimes wonder what happened to all my smoking, drinking, carousing friends.

I now note that smoking is injurious to my health. The surgeon general says so on every packet of cigarettes. In fact, the American Medical Association reports, "Cigarette smoking causes more premature deaths each year than . . . AIDS, fire, cocaine, car accidents, heroin, homicide, alcohol, suicide . . . put together" (*Journal of the American Medical Association:* 258, no. 15).

The April 18, 1994, issue of *U.S. News & World Report* reported in a segment entitled "The Reach and the Toll of Tobacco":

> Total annual number of tobacco-related deaths: 419,000
> Of those, cardiovascular disease deaths: 180,000
> Lung cancer deaths: 120,000
> Annual number of deaths from secondhand smoke:
> 9,000

I'm glad I never started! And I'm glad I didn't listen to my friends.

In regard to the issue of drinking, which, in the circles I was required to move, was considered a rite of passage, a badge of manhood, I now hear athletes and actors, businessmen and wives of presidents, the rich and famous, and the poor and unknown bemoaning their alcohol-induced fate and seeking help. One celebrity openly admitted that under the influence he'd "go from jocose to amorous and then to bellicose and then lachrymose and finally comatose."

The state of Wisconsin, where my family and I have made our home and established the center of our ministry for more than twenty-five years, has an unenviable record when it

---

TO HATE EVIL DOES NOT
MEAN TO HATE IT
SELECTIVELY, BUT TO BE
OPEN TO SEEING EVIL IN
ALL ITS MANIFESTATIONS
AND FROM THE DIVINE
PERSPECTIVE.

---

comes to alcohol. The U.S. Center for Disease Control reported in 1987 that in Wisconsin alcohol was the fourth leading cause of death after heart disease, cancer, and stroke. It was also reported that alcohol was a major factor in no fewer than 258 traffic deaths and that we led the nation in

1. binge drinking—5+ drinks on one occasion
2. chronic drinking—60+ drinks a month
3. drinking and driving

The Center also reported that even though the official drinking age was twenty-one, no less than 81 percent of young people between the ages of twelve and seventeen had consumed alcohol. I'm glad I never started that either!

Then there's the issue of sex before and outside of marriage. One of today's biggest issues is "safe sex." The reason for this is the prevalence of what we politely call STDs—sexually transmitted diseases. If you have sex with someone, you might catch what they've got, they having caught it from someone else, who got it from someone else! I spoke recently with a missionary doctor who has devoted his life to caring for the poor people of São Paulo, Brazil. He told me that he regularly spends approximately one hour with each patient, dealing not only with their medical symptoms but with the underlying causes of their maladies. But when he deals with STDs he traces meticulously all the sexual partners from whom and to whom the diseases have passed. An impossible task in São Paulo and, I might add, in North America too. No wonder people are running scared and going in for "safe sex," as if there were such a thing. Well, actually there is! It's the old-fashioned approach that the Bible teaches and my fundamentalist heritage taught: no sex outside of marriage.

Truly the fear of the Lord is a fountain of life that turns us from the snares of death; it is a secure fortress; and it does teach us to hate evil. And it is the beginning of wisdom—the fundamental basis of a system of values.

FIVE

MARRIAGES ARE MADE IN HEAVEN . . . BUT LIVED ELSEWHERE!

ABOUT fifty years after the American Republic was founded, French philosopher and sociologist Alexis de Tocqueville came to see firsthand the remarkable sociological experiment called the United States of America. Then he went home and wrote a book called *Democracy in America,* which as far as I can tell is more often quoted than read. Be that as it may, along with many other insightful observations he said:

> Certainly of all countries in the world, America is the one in which the marriage tie is most respected and where the highest and truest conception of conjugal happiness has been conceived. (Doubleday, Anchor Books, 1969, 291)

High praise indeed!

Many years later the United States Supreme Court handed down an opinion that included the following statement:

> Marriage is an institution in whose maintenance and purity the public is deeply interested for it is the

foundation of the family and society without which there would be neither civilization nor progress.

I think it would be true to say that in light of what de Tocqueville had to say about the early days of the American Republic and what, in subsequent years, the Supreme Court stated, we need to be asking some serious questions, such as, What happened?

America now leads the Western democracies in divorce. At least 50 percent of new marriages end in divorce. The National Association of Evangelicals reported in its September 1992 newsletter that, since 1960, teen sexual activity has doubled, cohabitation has increased by 600 percent, illegitimate births have increased by more than 500 percent, teen suicides have tripled, and the American Psychological Association has rated "decline of the nuclear family as the number one threat to mental health." Would de Tocqueville recognize America if he returned today? How could social mores change so drastically?

Social Values Lead to Social Condition

I believe these social changes are due to changes in our values as a society, and I am not alone in this opinion. While the America that de Tocqueville visited could not accurately be described as a Christian nation, biblical values were in fact widely respected and in many instances deeply revered. But that is no longer the case. Secularization has taken over, and this is particularly true in attitudes toward marriage and family. But what does that mean? Carl F. H. Henry has written:

> Instead of recognizing Yahweh as the source and
> stipulator of truth and the good, contemporary
> thought reduces all reality to impersonal processes and
> events, and insists that man, himself, creatively imposes
> upon the Cosmos and upon history the only values that

they will ever bear. This dethronement of God and enthronement of man as lord of the universe, this eclipse of the supernatural and exaggeration of the natural, has precipitated an intellectual and moral crisis that escorts Western civilization, despite its brilliant technological achievements, ever nearer to anguished collapse and atheistic suffocation. (*The Christian Mindset in a Secular Society,* Multnomah Press, 1984, 84)

Secularization is what happens when humans refuse to fear the Lord or recognize Yahweh as the source and stipulator of truth. They then creatively impose their own values on their world. In order to do this, they have to work from their own set of assumptions. There's nothing wrong with working from assumptions unless, of course, the assumptions are wrong. And on the subject of marriage and family, secular thought holds some basic assumptions that are seriously questionable, two of the major ones being (1) marriage was a human idea—something that human beings dreamed up as they developed in their relational skills and addressed the problems of living in society, and (2) societies go through evolutionary processes.

ON THE SUBJECT OF MARRIAGE AND FAMILY, SECULAR THOUGHT HOLDS SOME BASIC ASSUMPTIONS THAT ARE SERIOUSLY QUESTIONABLE.

We will prove later in the chapter that marriage was conceived first of all by God, our Creator. As to the evolution of marriage and family, we need to divide this assumption into its subassumptions. When people say that marriage has evolved, they are usually assuming that evolution produces advanced states, and therefore any changes in the structures of marriages and families must by definition be an advance, an improvement.

This line of reasoning leads to the conclusion that in America's early days the old approach to marriage and family was perfectly appropriate, but in the modern era it has been superseded by "alternative lifestyles," which in secular thought are not only perfectly legitimate but are probably an improvement on what used to be.

Maris Vinovskis, a professor at the University of Michigan, was quoted by *Time* magazine in a special fall 1992 issue as saying, "The fact of change is the one constant throughout the history of the family. The family is the most flexible adaptive institution. It is constantly evolving."

Once it is assumed that marriage and the family are purely human ideas, there will be no restraints on human attempts to improve these societal structures. Andrea Engber is convinced that she had a very good reason for coming up with what she is convinced is a better alternative than marriage. She is a single mother who admitted that she was "living with a guy that I didn't want to marry" and said, "I stayed with him because I wanted a child. But I didn't want him." After the child was born, she lost her job, so she started a magazine called *SingleMOTHER* in order that "women in my position could support each other." She added, "I wouldn't change anything I've done. You only have to look at the divorce rate to see that *marriage isn't working.*" (italics added) (*First*, 19 October 1992). Her reason for an alternative? Marriage isn't working. Her solution? Single parenthood.

But saying that marriage isn't working is benign stuff compared to much of the rhetoric that many influential people are leveling at this ancient institution. In a "World Report" dated

March 28, 1994, and entitled "The War against Women," *U.S. News & World Report* documented instances of female victimization from around the world. The article noted approvingly that "the 1993 U.N. Human Development Report found that there still is no country that treats its women as well as its men." We don't have to be radical feminists to know that there is a lot of truth to that statement. It is not too difficult to understand, either, why the U.N. is sponsoring a fourth women's conference in Beijing, according to the article, for the purpose of "righting the wrongs against the second sex. High among them is what Health and Human Services Secretary Donna Shalala calls *'terrorism in the home'*" (italics added).

MANY A SMILING FACE
HIDES A BREAKING HEART
AND MANY A DESIGNER
JACKET, A BROKEN RIB.

I have been a pastor long enough to know that there are many marriages that look perfectly normal on the outside but are actually desperately dysfunctional. Many a smiling face hides a breaking heart and many a designer jacket, a broken rib. *Terrorism in the home* is a highly emotive phrase, but it may be an apt description of the things that are being done by some people to their marriage partners.

So two of the main reasons we are given for the desire to bring about changes in the institutions of marriage and family are that it isn't working and that marriage in some way lends itself to the violation of women, and occasionally men. Therefore, on both counts, "marriage is broken—let's fix it. Marriage and family have always changed, so let's bring about some more changes."

Changing Definitions of Marriage and Family

We can certainly acknowledge that the family has seen dramatic changes during the course of human history. In the beginning there was a family—Adam and Eve and their boys—which, in modern parlance, was extremely dysfunctional! As time went on, the emphasis seemed to be placed on clans and tribes, then extended families. Obviously there were changes even in biblical times. More recently, in fact, since the Industrial Revolution, we have become familiar with the nuclear family—the Ozzie and Harriet model. Family structures have changed over the years for various sociological, economic, and geographical reasons.

In the same way it is clear that attitudes toward marriage have changed. Even in biblical history we can see that first there was monogamy, then polygamy, then the introduction of concubines, and with these changes came all kinds of problems. So we can agree that there have been changes in the structures of marriage and family down through the centuries. But we need not subscribe to the theory that marriage is a human idea and that it is evolving in increasingly better forms. But that, of course, is exactly what secularists are saying and what they want us to believe. The *Time* magazine article already cited stated this point of view quite bluntly:

> It is reasonable to ask whether in the future there will be a family at all. Given the propensity for divorce, the growing number of adults who choose to remain single, the declining popularity of having children, and the evaporation of the time families spend together, another way may eventually evolve. In any event, as the nuclear family dissolves what is likely to evolve is a sort of make your own family approach. . . . The family of choice.

Not everybody is as prepared to write off marriage and the family as *Time,* even though people are eagerly looking for ways to fix what they perceive to be the problems in the old institutions. Some of them have adopted the much more subtle but no less challenging approach of simply redefining the institutions. So instead of the traditional definition of a family which is "two or more persons related by birth, marriage, or adoption and residing together," they are advocating defining the family as "a group of people who love and care for each other."

WILL GETTING RID OF
COMMITMENT IN SOME WAY
CAUSE PEOPLE TO BE MORE
WARM AND INTIMATE?

Notice the emphasis on love and care. Who could quarrel with that? But why the refusal to incorporate commitment? The reasoning behind this is very easy to see. In previous generations there was a solid commitment to marriage, but often it was a commitment seriously lacking in love and caring intimacy. There was often bitterness and much suppressed anger and icy isolation within "committed" marriages. Many younger people observing this in their parents' marriages have said, "No way am I going to get myself into a situation like that. If that's what the institution of marriage does for you, who needs it? What we need is warmth. What we need is intimacy. And if we can't find warmth and intimacy inside these cold, bitter, icy institutions, then we'll think of something better." While we can readily sympathize with the concerns of these people, we have to question their naive assumption that getting rid of commitment will in some way cause people to be more warm and intimate.

We share the genuine concern of those who have been damaged by the institution of marriage. But we are also left with the uneasy feeling that there are underlying motives for rejecting marriage—motives that are not always voiced. We can give people like Tanya Tucker credit at least for their honesty when they make such statements as, "I'd be divorced four times by now if I'd gotten married. I don't want to answer to any guy. Even though I'm a single mother, I don't feel lonely. I just pray I make the right decisions when it comes to my kids." (*First,* 19 Oct. 1992).

And Irving Kristol says bluntly:

> Only in Hollywood, where the lingua franca is sociobabble and psychobabble, or in the barren wastes of academia does one hear about "alternative families." Even there it is but a sly attempt to legitimate homosexual liaisons. (*Wall Street Journal,* 7 Dec. 1992)

So whether we sympathize with the concerns of young people who distrust marriage because of what they have seen in the marriages of their parents, or whether we suspect what Kristol suspects and accept what Tucker admits, we still must wonder what kind of glorious confusion would reign if, in the midst of our personal confusion and the variety of our sources and opinions, we sought to "fix what's broke" in marriage by redefining it completely!

For instance, try to understand what Garth Brooks, the famous country and Western singer, said when he responded to a question about his apparent affirmation of same-sex marriages in his song "We Shall Be Free." He "clarified" his position by stating, "It's tough for me because I love the Bible. For those people that feel religiously that homosexuality is wrong, are they not as right as the people who feel homosexuality is right?" ("Garth Takes a Brave Stand," *Newsweek,* 12 Oct. 1992). How's that for confusion?

So where does this leave us?

I suggest that we need to admit that there have been historical changes in human approaches to marriage and family; that these changes have not by any stretch of the imagination led to an evolution of something superior to what was known before; and that it is a serious error to assume that marriage and family are simply human inventions that can be changed by human beings without any repercussions to our individual and community lives. Granted there are serious problems in marriages

IT IS A SERIOUS ERROR TO ASSUME THAT MARRIAGE AND FAMILY ARE SIMPLY HUMAN INVENTIONS THAT WE CAN CHANGE WITHOUT ANY REPERCUSSIONS TO OUR LIVES.

and families, but to discredit the institutions because of the problems is similar to the attempt of some British intellectuals to discredit the church because of World War I—a position that led G. K. Chesterton to comment, "They might as well say that the Ark was discredited by the Flood." He went on to explain, "When the world goes wrong, it proves rather that the church is right. The church is justified, not because her children do not sin, but because they do" (*The Everlasting Man,* London: Hodder and Stoughton, 1934, 3–4).

In the same way we should take the position that the institutions of marriage and family, far from being discredited by their sinful abuse, are proven to be the right way to go because when adhered to according to divine principles, they have proved to be the greatest antidote to man's innate proclivity to abusive behavior in relationships.

Let's remind ourselves of some of Proverbs' "family values," with special reference to marriage.

Tried and True Statements about Marriage

There is nothing new about marriage being under attack. The Proverbs give powerful teaching on the subject of defending against the forces that would seek to undo the marital bond. Note how wisdom—values from the sovereign Lord—serves in this capacity:

> *Wisdom will save you from the ways of wicked men,*
> *from men whose words are perverse,*
> *who leave the straight paths*
> *to walk in dark ways. . . .*
> *It will save you also from the adulteress,*
> *from the wayward wife with her seductive words,*
> *who has left the partner of her youth*
> *and ignored the covenant she made before God.*
> Proverbs 2:12-13, 16-17

We have already considered much of what could be described as "perverse words" from those "who leave the straight paths to walk in dark ways." The abuse of marriage is described in these verses as well. A person has "left the partner of her youth and ignored the covenant she made before God." This is not to suggest for a moment that all marital breakdown can or should be laid at the feet of women! One charge fits all. Notice how these charges give us clues to the basic values that God ascribes to marriage.

Marriage as sacred covenant

The word *covenant* is not used much today, so we need to be clear on its significance in this context. The unique relationship that existed between Israel and Jehovah was based on a covenant that he had initiated with Abram. Called by the Lord from the relative comfort of his home in Ur of the Chaldees, with nothing more to go on than a promise that he would be shown where to go and that he would be blessed when he got there, Abram went! The land to which he went was inhabited by people who were intent on staying there. Nevertheless, Jehovah made a covenant with Abram that stipulated, "To your descendants I give this land" (Genesis 15:18). Later on, when Abram, a.k.a. Abraham, was ninety-nine years old, Jehovah confirmed the covenant, saying among other things:

> *"I will establish my covenant as an everlasting covenant*
> *between me and you and your descendants after you for*
> *the generations to come, to be your God and the God of*
> *your descendants after you. The whole land of Canaan,*
> *where you are now an alien, I will give as an everlasting*
> *possession to you and your descendants after you; and I*
> *will be their God." Then God said to Abraham, "As for*
> *you, you must keep my covenant, you and your*
> *descendants after you for the generations to come."*
> Genesis 17:7-9

The idea of covenant was as ingrained in the Israelite mindset as the concept of constitution is ingrained in the American. Without the covenant there would have been no Israel, as without the Constitution there would be no United States. Every Israelite knew that the nation operated under the covenant; every young Israelite was raised from his earliest years with that understanding. All that they were and all that they had and all that they ever hoped to be was wrapped up in the covenant. Jehovah had chosen them to be his people for his own reasons and purposes; he had staked his reputation on being their God and delivering on his promises; and all he asked of them was that they respond by being his people and living according to the covenant. No Israelite would misunderstand the meaning of covenant.

So when they embarked on marriage they made a covenant within a covenant. Every part of Israelite life was covenant structured, and on that basis they made another covenant. They understood that marriage was God's idea, not man's. They recognized that it was to be lived out God's way, not theirs. They knew that covenants involved promises and commitments, and they went ahead and made them in a covenant to each other based on the ancient statement God had made right at the beginning of human history: "For this reason a man will leave his father and mother and be united to his wife, and they will become one flesh" (Gen. 2:24).

But the Israelites were far from perfect, which meant they had less-than-perfect marriages. So Jehovah sent his prophets at regular intervals to remind them about the covenant he had made with them and the covenants they had made with each other before him. For example, when the people complained that their worship of the Lord was becoming meaningless, Malachi told them:

> You weep and wail because [God] no longer pays
> attention to your offerings or accepts them with pleasure
> from your hands. You ask, "Why?" It is because the Lord is
> acting as the witness between you and the wife of your
> youth, because you have broken faith with her, though she
> is your partner, the wife of your marriage covenant. Has
> not the Lord made them one? In flesh and spirit they are
> his. And why one? Because he was seeking godly offspring.

So guard yourself in your spirit, and do not break faith with the wife of your youth. Malachi 2:13-15

One Plus One = One

When two people are married in church by a minister, they are tacitly saying, "We want to be married in church by a minister because we recognize the divine dimension of marriage. We are making a covenant before God. We've got our witnesses who'll sign the marriage contract. Our friends and relatives are

WHEN TWO PEOPLE ARE ONE "IN SPIRIT," IT MEANS SOMETHING FAR BEYOND HAVING SEX.

here to witness our covenant promises. But more important, God is our witness. We are making this solemn covenant commitment to each other before the Lord."

But there is more. When we make a covenant before God, something is done to us *by* God. And what is that? He takes two very different people, and in some remarkable way he makes them one. Remember Malachi's words, "Has not the Lord made them one? In flesh and in spirit they are his." To make two people one "in spirit" is different from making them one "in flesh." Put in very simple terms, when two people become one "in flesh," it means they have sex. But when two people are one "in spirit," it means something far beyond having sex. It means God is binding their two lives together so that over the years, as they pass through changing circumstances, they will discover a oneness of spirit that enables them to respond in ways that serve only to deepen their love and commitment to each other. They become more and more deeply integrated into each other's personalities. They begin to see things through each other's eyes. They instinctively think each other's thoughts. My wife even finishes my sentences for me—not always the way I intended, but sometimes better than I could have done it!

One of the ways in which this oneness of spirit is demonstrated is in the oneness of sexual enjoyment of each other. These two forms of oneness are related; they must not be divorced from each other. It is therefore utterly wrong to be joined sexually with someone to whom one has not been joined spiritually. It is equally wrong for people to be joined spiritually but not to enjoy being joined together in healthy matrimonial sex. So the marriage covenant is a commitment we make before God, which introduces us to something that is done to us by God.

But we may ask with Malachi, "Why one?" or Why does God do this? Why is he so concerned about male/female relationships that he should outline principles of behavior for them and even be involved in making them unique? The prophet's answer is what we need to hear: "because he was seeking godly offspring." I am painfully aware that there are large numbers of young couples who are struggling with infertility problems. I don't want to say anything that will add to their pain. But I'm sure they will understand when I say, "All things being equal, when God joins two people together in spirit and they come together in flesh, there will be offspring." Why we have such a high incidence of infertility in our Western culture I would not want to speculate, but apparently it has something to do with the fallenness of our physical beings and the resultant fallenness of the environment we have created. All we can say is, ideally, in the coming together of spirit and flesh through divine covenant, the result is offspring, which the parents have the responsibility to bring up in the fear and admonition of the

Lord. This is what true wisdom teaches. These are the core values—the basis of family values.

The ancient Israelites, not unlike the modern people of the industrialized Western democracies, had strayed far from these principles. Not a few were like the woman who had left the partner of her youth and ignored the covenant she made before God. Malachi needed to remind the Israelites that, even though in Moses' day the Lord had reluctantly allowed divorce in limited circumstances because of the hardness of the people's hearts, his position was, "I hate divorce . . . and I hate a man's covering himself [or 'his wife,' NIV margin] with violence as well as with his garment" (Mal. 2:16). Note that the Lord not only hates to see people breaking a covenant they made before him, but he also hates the kind of violent behavior that leads to this kind of breakdown. It isn't so much divorce that's the problem, as the godless, ill-disciplined behavior that violates the spouse and leads to the breakdown of trust, care, and mutual concern, which so often ends in divorce. My daughter, Judy Golz, in a doctoral dissertation submitted to New York University, came up with ample empirical evidence that the

THE GREATER PROBLEM IS THE GODLESS, ILL-DISCIPLINED BEHAVIOR THAT VIOLATES FAMILY MEMBERS AND LEADS TO THE BREAKDOWN OF TRUST, CARE, AND MUTUAL CONCERN, WHICH SO OFTEN ENDS IN DIVORCE.

damage done to young people in intact but abusive families is not measurably different from that done to young people through the tragedy of divorce. It isn't just divorce that God hates—it's the kind of behavior that so often leads to divorce.

Marriage as companionship

This Malachi passage says that the man has left his partner in the marriage covenant. Note the word translated "partner." It occurs on numerous occasions throughout Proverbs, often translated "friend." So for example, Proverbs 17:17 states, "A friend loves at all times," and Proverbs 18:24, "There is a friend who sticks closer than a brother." In other words, marriage is intended to be a companionship of two people who stick closer than anybody else to each other—who genuinely love at all times. It is a companionship of mutual caring. Proverbs 27:6 gives us another clue about this kind of friendship, reminding us, "Wounds from a friend can be trusted," while Proverbs 27:9 adds, "The pleasantness of one's friend springs from his earnest counsel." In other words, marriage is a relationship in which two friends come together, care for each other, confront each other to build each other up, and counsel each other, in order that there might be growth as individuals and growth together. That's what marriage is intended to be. It is covenant. It is companionship.

Now, sad to say, some purely secular marriages appear to understand this better than many Christian marriages. Recently I read a beautiful description of this kind of marital companionship in a most unexpected place—*Esquire* magazine, which is not the source you usually go to, to find an illustration of marital bliss, Christian or otherwise! Author Irwin Shaw described his marriage in the following terms: "Mutual and unexpressed understanding, private jokes, comfort in adversity, automatic support in times of trouble, and hours spent in cordial silence and tranquil evenings" (July 1989, 73).

I'm sure that many people read those words wistfully, wondering what happened to their marriages, which are so lacking in anything remotely like this kind of companionship. It could be that they never understood that marriages, like friendships, require work. Marriage companionship over the years, like lasting friendships, takes time to develop.

Marriage as commitment
The fifth chapter of Proverbs contains unambiguous wisdom—values—for young (and old) people who find themselves in tempting situations. And who doesn't in this world?

> *Keep to a path far from her,*
> *do not go near the door of her house,*
> *lest you give your best strength to others*
> *and your years to one who is cruel,*
> *lest strangers feast on your wealth*
> *and your toil enrich another man's house.*
> Proverbs 5:8-10

If I didn't know better, I would think that the author of these proverbs had gone through the American divorce courts, where he came up against a slick attorney who took him to the cleaners! The kind of situation where a man goes through a divorce, loses home and family, and drives to work past his old home each morning, where his former wife is now living happily ever after with her new partner. Gritting his teeth, he drives on to work to earn money so that a stranger can feast on his wealth, ruefully remembering that it was his own infidelity that drove his wife into the other man's arms and his wealth eventually into another man's pocket.

Good advice comes in both negative and positive forms. We've seen the negative; now look at the positive:

Drink water from your own cistern,
running water from your own well.
Should your springs overflow in the streets,
your streams of water in the public squares?
Let them be yours alone,
never to be shared with strangers.
May your fountain be blessed,
and may you rejoice in the wife of your youth.
Proverbs 5:15-18

There is a very definite sense of commitment here. It's *your own* cistern and *your own* well. Let them be *yours alone.* Never to be shared with strangers. May *your* fountain be blessed, and may you rejoice in *the wife of your youth.* Marriage is covenant. Marriage is companionship. Marriage is commitment. Commitment establishes marital foundations, and it builds in its own limits. There's a commitment to a relationship into which nobody else is allowed to intrude. This intimacy is preserved by refusing to take it outside the limits of the marital relationship. And these limits are designed to create an area in which an extraordinarily loving commitment might be nurtured and nourished.

One lovely summer day Jill and I got up early to get our morning exercise. Jill walks two miles around our lake in a clockwise direction. I run around it twice in a counterclockwise direction. I suppose you could say that's a picture of our marriage; she walks and I run, and we go in opposite directions! But as I was running and saw her in the distance walking toward me I thought how special she is to me, and as I passed her I said, "I love you." It seemed perfectly appropriate. I kept running; she kept walking, but as I passed her the second time I added, "And I still love you!" She laughed and kept on walking. I laughed and kept on running, and nobody watching would have known our intimate secret, but they would have seen two happy people enjoying each other. For thirty-six-plus years that has been the basis of our marriage.

Earlier in the chapter we noted some of the less-than-acceptable attitudes toward marriage that are being voiced and demonstrated by many of our celebrities. In all fairness we need to note that there are glowing exceptions. Actor Paul Newman is one. Somewhere I came across this quote of a statement he made on the sixtieth birthday of his wife, Joanne Woodward, after they had been married thirty-two years:

THE DAMAGE DONE TO YOUNG PEOPLE IN INTACT BUT ABUSIVE FAMILIES IS NOT MEASURABLY DIFFERENT FROM THAT DONE TO YOUNG PEOPLE THROUGH DIVORCE.

I feel privileged to love that woman. The fact that I am married to her is the single greatest joy of my life. Joanne is fascinating to me, and always will be. We live in a throwaway society. We throw away bottles and cans, children, careers and marriages. Joanne and I work at mending things. We fix the toaster when it breaks, and likewise we fix our marriage when it is strained.

This from a man surrounded by Hollywood's beautiful young things, rich and powerful, attractive and highly successful. Yet he says that his marriage to a sixty-year-old woman is "the single greatest joy of my life"! So all is not lost.

Malachi shall have the last word in this chapter: "So guard yourself in your spirit, and do not break faith with the wife of your youth."

Apparently he wasn't sure the people were listening so he then added, "So guard yourself in your spirit, and do not break faith."

SIX

IF YOU VALUE YOUR CHILDREN, TEACH THEM VALUES

A TEENAGE son and his father were having a difference of opinion. In exasperation the boy exploded, "I didn't ask to be born into this family!" To which his father replied, "You're right, and if you had, the answer would have been no!" It is possible that, on reflection, the father might have modified his response, but there was no need for the boy to alter his position—although his attitude could no doubt have improved!

It is true that children are born, not because of their desire, but because of the action of their parents. This clearly places maximum responsibility for the child's well-being on those whose actions, from a human point of view, brought about his or her existence. And since a male and a female are necessary for producing the child, it would seem logical that—ideally—a male parent and a female parent would accept the privilege and responsibility of caring for the child they have produced.

I am careful to say ideally because there are many wonderful parents who, for reasons outside their control, find themselves struggling to raise children on their own without the benefit of a spouse. My own father was brought up by his gentle, sweet mother and his strong grandmother after his father died when my father was a young boy. And some of the most impressive young people I know are those who have been deserted by their former spouses and left to bring up children, often without even receiving the financial support to which they are entitled.

It Takes One Man and One Woman to Make One Child

With these exceptions in mind, it is still reasonable and logical to say that a child should have a parent of each sex, joined in the commitment of marriage, who will devote themselves to bringing up this child they have produced together. As simple and obvious as this is, it is not a unanimous position in our culture.

We've already mentioned the firestorm that engulfed the unfortunate Dan Quayle when he questioned the advisability of unmarried women bringing up children on their own. And increasingly we are seeing gays and lesbians, in their struggle to have their lifestyles accepted as normative, insisting that they should have full rights to adopt children and that their arrangement should be recognized as a family structure. Many of them, like one lesbian couple, both of whom are officers on the Boston police force, are making great efforts to show that the child they are bringing up will in no way be jeopardized, except perhaps, in their opinion, by the "bigotry" of those who disagree with their point of view. In an effort to ensure that young people brought up by gay or lesbian couples will not be ridiculed by their school friends, the New York Education Authority went to great trouble to produce books for students showing that there are different kinds of "families" and that we should be understanding and accept them. So it is easy to see that what has been the obvious way of looking at family is not so obvious—or so simple—anymore.

President Johnson, speaking at Howard University in 1965, said, "The family is a cornerstone of our society. More than any other force it shapes the attitudes, the hopes, the ambitions, and the values of the child. When the family collapses, it is the children that are usually damaged. When it happens on a massive scale, the community itself is crippled."

At first sight, a quotation like this would encourage us, because Washington is aware of the problem, is firmly on the side of the family, and will come up with some solutions. But look again. Such is the struggle in high places on this subject that when the Carter administration called a White House conference on families in 1980, they achieved very little because the time was spent quarreling over what exactly constitutes a family! Those who assumed that they were going to discuss ways of helping Mom and Dad cope with the pressures of bringing up Johnny and Jenny in their home in the sub-

---

SOME PARENTS STEER THEIR
CHILDREN IN A CERTAIN
DIRECTION BECAUSE THEY
WERE NEVER ALLOWED TO
GO THAT WAY THEMSELVES.

---

urbs, while caring for a dog and a cat and watching one and a half television sets, were in for a rude awakening. To their horror and amazement, they found themselves confronted by groups of outspoken people who insisted on a definition of family that would not only recognize that their particular brand of cohabitation was common but that it was also normative and must therefore be given equal status with "the traditional family." While they were surprised and dismayed, their opponents were incensed and infuriated that they encountered resistance from the traditionalists, whom they dismissed as zealots and bigots.

Barbara Dafoe Whitehead, in a startling article in *Atlantic Monthly* magazine entitled "Dan Quayle Was Right" wrote,

"Every time the issue of family structure has been raised the response has been first controversy, then retreat, and finally silence" (April 1993). Wading into the controversy, armed with a mass of evidence from social science research, Whitehead took on the naysayers who had derided the former vice president.

> The human child is born in an abjectly helpless and immature state. Years of nurture and protection are needed before the child can achieve physical independence. Similarly, it takes years of interaction with at least one but ideally two or more adults for a child to develop into a socially competent adult. . . . The social arrangement that has proved most successful in ensuring the physical survival and promoting the social development of the child is the family unit of the biological mother and father.

While she limited her remarks to the physical and social realms, the same things could be said about the child's spiritual well-being. So while in Washington the politicians may not have the nerve to address the issue of family structure even though they are greatly concerned about the social and economic ramifications of family disintegration, there is no reason for Christians to retreat or remain silent, because the Scriptures are loud and clear on the subject.

As we look into the Scriptures we can discover not only what the issues are when we confront those who no longer accept what the Bible teaches on the family, but we will also be clear in our minds what family values are, particularly as they relate to bringing up children in a confused environment. Once again we will turn to the book of Proverbs.

> *Train a child in the way he should go, and when he is old he will not turn from it.* Proverbs 22:6

Some people take this as a cast-iron promise. They reason, *God says if I raise my kids as they ought to be raised, while they might deviate from my principles for a period, in the end they'll come around to the way I brought them up, and all will be well.* This understanding has brought a considerable amount of comfort to godly parents who have watched their youngsters go off to college and go off the rails at the same time. But they have held on to the promise even when their children, who are no longer kids, persist in behavior patterns that are far removed from those they learned at their mother's knee.

> IF PARENTS WANT THEIR CHILDREN TO TAKE SPIRITUAL MATTERS SERIOUSLY, THEY MUST MAKE SPIRITUAL CONCERNS A PRIORITY IN THEIR OWN LIVES.

Other people say, "No, there is no written guarantee here that the children of godly parents will always turn out to be godly. The facts clearly point in a different direction, and hard as it is for some of us to accept, this is not a *promise;* it is a *proverb.*"

Proverbs are pithy sayings that are generally true. For example, "Like father, like son" is generally true, but all of us know exceptions. "Forewarned is forearmed" is often very true, but there are too many examples of the forewarned who chose not to be forearmed, whose wreckage litters human history. What then is the value of the statement, "Train a child in the way he should go, and when he is old he will not turn from it"?

Who Decides the "Should"

Should is the operative word here. Who decides the "should" for a child? Our first response would be to name the parents as those who set the direction for their child. And many parents do determine what their kids should be and what they should do. They feel that these children have come into their orbit of influence, that they are going to care for these children, and that part of that care is helping the child find a direction and go that way.

The book of Proverbs assumes that godly parents will endeavor to bring up godly children. But there are parents who go far beyond the designs of godliness for their children. Some put great pressure on their youngsters concerning where they should live and the details of their lifestyle. Some parents decide that their children should go to a particular school. In England (and here in America, too, I'm told) some parents sign their child up for entry into the school they themselves attended—as soon as the child is born! If the question is asked, "Why this school?" the only reason is, "Because that's the school I went to." Some people decide that their children should go into a certain career. The reason? Because the family has been in this particular business for years, and the tradition must be carried on, or because the father has invested his life in creating the business, and he wants nothing more than to bequeath it to his children. My father worked very hard to build up a grocery business during the Depression and World War II years in Britain, and he wanted me to take over the business. But I had no interest and less desire, and he, fortunately, did not attempt to determine the "should" for me based on his own desires.

Sometimes there's a more subtle motivation. Parents have been known to steer their children in a certain direction because they were never allowed to go that way themselves. For years they have been resentful that they missed their life's dream, and they are determined that their children get the chance that they missed—whether the children want it or not. This kind of drive in the parent often hurts more than it helps in the development of that child.

I have a friend whose father was a successful dentist, so he gained the impression that he should be a dentist, and for years he was a good one if not a very happy one. But he eventually

THERE ARE PARENTS WHO GO BEYOND GODLY LEADERSHIP; THEY PUT GREAT PRESSURE ON THEIR YOUNGSTERS CONCERNING THE DETAILS OF THEIR LIFESTYLE.

sold his dental practice and became a landscape gardener, and he has never been more fulfilled. My daughter was convinced that I wanted her to be a surgeon, and so she applied herself to her premed studies assiduously, winning the prize for top student during her junior year. But she was never comfortable with the peculiar pressures that medicine places on women who want to be wives and mothers as well as professionals. Actually, I had no such aspirations for her, and it was only after she became ill with anorexia nervosa that we discovered the misunderstanding and relieved the pressure. She went on to be a very fulfilled young Ph.D. in a totally different discipline, as well as a wife and mother.

Who then determines the "should"? If it isn't the parent, is it the child? Anyone who knows anything about children knows that they rarely know what they want to be when they grow up even though well-meaning grown-ups insist on asking them. My wife, Jill, was eating dinner with a couple she had known since they were teenagers and was enjoying getting to know their children. The youngest was not getting a word in edgewise, so Jill asked him the inevitable question: "And what do you want to be when you grow up?" He was momentarily overwhelmed at being recognized, but after careful thought he said, "Bigger!" That's probably as far as most kids can safely project, although there are rare exceptions where youngsters know early on which way they want to go. But one can hardly leave young children alone to determine the "should" of their lives. If not the parents and the child, then who? That becomes the crucial question. Who determines the "should"?

We need to remember that Proverbs was written in the context of the covenant God had established with his people. The ancient people of Israel believed that the Lord had a plan for their lives. He had made that clear to Abraham and had reaffirmed it at regular intervals. That being the case, they had no difficulty recognizing that the Lord had plans for individuals. They believed that the Lord in his sovereignty had given attributes, abilities, and aptitudes to the child that, when developed, would show quite clearly what the child should be and do. For them it was clear that the Lord decided the "should." But if that was the case, what was the role of the parent? *The task of the parent was, and is, to embark, with the child, on an exploration of what God had in mind when he brought that child into the world and gave him to the parents to bring up.*

Helping Your Child Discover God's Plan

In times of war naval vessels sometimes used to set out to sea without anyone on board having a clear idea of where they were going. For security reasons, the captain would have instructions to proceed to a certain point. When they had reached that point, he and the first officer would go to the ship's safe, and together they would take out the sealed envelope in which the details of their mission were outlined. They had sailed from port under what were known as "sealed orders." The mission had already been determined, but they only discovered it after they had set sail.

I believe that children sail into life under sealed orders. The task of the parent, along with the child, is to break the seal and find out what God had in mind when he brought this child into existence. Together, parent and child discover the "should."

> CHILDREN SAIL INTO LIFE UNDER SEALED ORDERS. THE TASK OF PARENT AND CHILD IS TO BREAK THE SEAL AND FIND OUT WHAT GOD HAD IN MIND WHEN HE BROUGHT THIS CHILD INTO EXISTENCE.

The question is, How do parents go about this high-sounding task?

The power of dedicating your child to the Lord

It is helpful to notice that the word *train* can also mean "dedicate" or "inaugurate." In the same way that buildings are dedicated or inaugurated when they are completed and ready for occupancy, so parents set the child on the right course, inaugurating the process of discovering and doing God's will. If a child is dedicated to the Lord and the parents are dedicated to bringing that child up to be what he or she was dedicated to be, then they are very likely to discover together the "should" that God has in mind for the child. And the child who has been told that the parents have committed themselves to discovering God's plans for him or her is likely to become intrigued by that thought and grow interested in joining the adventure.

Recently I received a copy of a book called *In the Heart of Savagedom,* for which I have been looking for many years. Shortly before I was born my father was reading this book. It was written by Mrs. Stuart Watt and tells the story of her and Mr. Watt's incredibly courageous missionary ventures more than a hundred years ago into what they called "the heart of savagedom"—in what we now call Zaire. My father was so impressed by this couple that he looked up from his reading and said to my mother, who was about to produce me, "If this child's a boy, his name is Stuart!"

I am now sixty-three years of age, but I have eagerly looked for a copy of that book for a long time because I wanted to read for myself what had impressed my father so much that he had wanted to dedicate me to its message. Every time I think about how I got my name, I think of missions and ministry, so it's not really surprising that I turned out the way that I did! There's no guarantee that dedicating a child will always bring this sort of result, but it is obvious that this kind of action on the part of a parent, along with the work of God's grace, will have a profound, positive effect on a child. "Train a child in the way he should go, and when he is old he will not turn from it" is a rule that is generally true. That's one reason we teach values to our children.

Setting a course to a good destination
The prologue to the book of Proverbs says:

> *[Proverbs are] for giving prudence to the simple,*
> *knowledge and discretion to the young.* 1:4

We've already looked into these words, *knowledge and discretion.* Together they mean developing perceptive, workable plans for life. So assuming that children are being steered in the way that they should go, they now need help getting there. It's one thing to help a young person discover God's purpose, but it's an entirely different thing to help him put it into practice. It is not uncommon for young people to have a theoretical concept of the divine will but to be sadly deficient in know-how as to what it looks like or how it works. Parents can help by modeling this process in their own lives and by surrounding the child with other positive role models. As I look back on my

IT'S ONE THING TO HELP A YOUNG PERSON DISCOVER GOD'S PURPOSE, BUT IT'S AN ENTIRELY DIFFERENT THING TO HELP HIM PUT IT INTO PRACTICE.

early childhood, there's absolutely no question in my mind that I am, to a very large extent, a reflection of the role models who surrounded me. These people were both interesting and attractive to me.

I think particularly of Captain Horace Sidney May of the Royal Artillery. He was every inch a soldier, unabashedly a Christian, helpful, friendly, cheerful, positive, open, interested in me—everything I thought a man should be! Long after I left England, he still wrote to me regularly in impeccable hand-writing—something he modeled that I have not emulated! His letters were invariably full of joy, brimming with vision, always positively looking for ways to make his life count for God. He told me he listened regularly to my radio broadcasts, and he frequently made suggestions about how they could be improved—and occasionally put my theology straight! He died a year or so ago, in his nineties. Even though I hadn't seen him for years, I experienced a deep sense of loss at his passing. Part of my life had passed on too.

I think of Harry Green. He was a very jovial bank manager. He's the one who steered me in the direction of a banking career, which I followed for twelve years. From him I learned that you could be an outspoken, outgoing Christian and a well-respected, highly efficient, thoroughly decent business-man. After I saw him in action, I knew that I wanted to be like him. You see, the task of the parent is to be instilling into the child both by verbal teaching and by positive models workable ways of getting where Junior is supposed to be. That is the task and the responsibility of parents.

Giving instruction on how to live with others

> *Listen, my son, to your father's instruction,*
> *and do not forsake your mother's teaching.*
> *They will be a garland to grace your head*
> *and a chain to adorn your neck.* Proverbs 1:8-9

Now this is poetic language, but the point is that father and mother, both of whom are involved in training and instructing the child, are doing so in order that the child develop a life "adorned" with gracious behavior. It's nice to meet well-be-haved kids. It's not a nice experience to meet brats who are an utter pain to themselves and everybody who has the misfortune of crossing their paths.

Now I'm not suggesting goody-two-shoes little kids. I like precocious, lively kids—kids who are pushing the limits, not because they have a rebellious spirit, but because they have a healthy spirit of adventure and discovery. I have three of my own, who are now busy producing at a phenomenal rate grandchildren of a similar disposition.

I got a great charge out of a kid who came to me one Sunday morning between services and said, "Well, Stuart, have you got anything significant to say this morning?" I knew exactly what his parents had been talking about in the car on the way to church!

IF THE KIDS OBSERVE THAT THEIR FAMILY WORSHIPS WHEN THERE'S NOTHING MORE EXCITING TO DO, THEY DECIDE THAT WORSHIP IS NOT VERY IMPORTANT.

One lovely summer's evening I was sitting at a Milwaukee Brewers baseball game across the aisle from a young family. The little boy was as obnoxious as his parents were oblivious. He was unruly and rude, blocking people's vision, refusing to sit down when asked, and generally making a nuisance of himself. All the time his parents acted as if he were on another planet. Perhaps they wished he were! At one point he threw some popcorn over the man sitting behind him, who had been trying to get the boy to sit down. The man turned to the little boy and said, "How old are you, son?"

The boy replied, "I'm seven. Who wants to know?"

The man responded, "Would you like to see eight?"

And I said, "Hallelujah!"

That little kid needed some major help, and he was getting absolutely none from his parents. They were producing by default a kid who was going to be a drag on society. We teach values to our children in order that, having ingrained them into their lives, they become a garland to grace their head and a chain to adorn their neck.

Being an involved parent

> *My son, if you accept my words*
> *and store up my commands within you,*
> *turning your ear to wisdom*
> *and applying your heart to understanding,*
> *and if you call out for insight*
> *and cry aloud for understanding,*
> *and if you look for it as for silver*
> *and search for it as for hidden treasure,*
> *then you will understand the fear of the Lord*
> *and find the knowledge of God.* Proverbs 2:1-5

Now notice that while this is a parent addressing a son, the word can also mean a child or a youth. It doesn't necessarily have to be masculine. The important thing is that a parent is addressing a young person on such significant topics as the fear of the Lord and the knowledge of God. In other words, here we have a parent teaching values that are rooted in deep spiritual realities.

One of the encouraging aspects of the boomer generation is that many of them, having adopted a certain lifestyle in the turbulent sixties, have decided they don't want their children to emulate their example. Remember the definition of a conservative: a liberal with teenage daughters! Many of them are returning to the church in order to give their children some moral teaching. This is good. But all too often they simply hand over their children to the professionals at church to provide for their spiritual needs in much the same way that they hand over their children to professional teachers to meet their educational needs and to the doctor to fix their physical problems. This approach has a certain logic, but it is inadequate from a spiritual perspective. By all means, parents should utilize the church's ministries as a supplement to their home teaching—but not as a substitute for parental spiritual input.

CHILDREN CAN WITHSTAND
A LOT OF PRESSURE AND
TRIAL FROM THE OUTSIDE IF
THE HOME INSIDE IS HELD
STEADY BY PARENTS WHOSE
CHARACTER IS STEADY.

Some years ago a popular song contained the helpful advice, "Don't send your kids to Sunday school; get out of bed and take 'em." If parents want their children to take spiritual matters seriously, they must make spiritual concerns a priority in their own lives. Young people have an unerring sense of justice, particularly when it comes to the way their parents treat them. They can smell an inconsistency a mile away and ferret it out with disconcerting skill. If kids know that Mom and Dad drop them off at Sunday school and then go off to drink coffee, they are quick to recognize the double standard. If the kids observe that their family worships when there's nothing more exciting to do, guess what? They decide that worship is not very important. Kids who never see their parents pray and never hear their parents read from God's Word find it hard to believe that prayer and Scripture are indispensable ingredients to balanced living. Wise parents know that if their children are to be what they were created to be they need consistent and constant spiritual oversight and encouragement at home.

The Value of Family Principles

Parenting with consistency can be such a challenging task that we err either by giving up on enforcing any rules or by burdening our children with far more rules than are necessary. When our three children were young, we adopted some basic principles concerning their spiritual development.

Family principle number one: This family believes in and practices daily devotions

There were times when we tried to have family devotions together. When the children were young it worked reasonably well, depending on how interesting we made the exercise. But once the children were adolescents, it became increasingly difficult to get everyone in the same place at the same time. Eventually we came to the conclusion that we shouldn't push it if it didn't work, if everybody became frustrated with everyone else in the name of worship! So to each child we gave devotional materials appropriate to his or her interests at the time, and we encouraged them to spend a few minutes in their own devotions every day. We kept an eye on them, assisting them as necessary. And it worked very well most of the time.

Family principle number two: This family worships regularly

We told our children, "Sunday mornings are for worship." Then we amplified the rule: "Wherever you are, whatever you're doing, whoever you're with, whatever your circumstances might be, Sunday morning is for worship, end of discussion." There were of course rare exceptions like fatal illness! Sunday evening services were optional. In those days we had a Sunday evening service. The option worked as follows: "If you can think of a valid reason you should not participate, then tell us about it, and we'll decide if it is valid or not." This retained parental authority but gave them a degree of freedom, and it taught them that freedom must be handled responsibly. In actual fact, it was a nonissue because most of their friends worshiped on Sunday evenings, and they wanted to be with their friends. Peer pressure at that stage of the game was more significant than parental pressure. That is why wise parents expose their children to healthy, positive peer pressure whenever possible.

Family principle number three: Members of this family will engage in at least one midweek spiritual activity of their choice each week
Each of our children chose entirely different activities, but while we made the rule, they made the choices—and stuck with them. They knew that when they arrived at the age of discretion (whenever that is!), they would make their own

NOT TO DISCIPLINE YOUR CHILD IS A DREADFULLY UNLOVING THING TO DO.

choices about spiritual involvement, but until that time we were, as parents, seriously endeavoring to teach them how to go about being and doing what God wanted them to be and do.

Children habitually "kick against the pricks" of much that their parents do, but wise parents accept this temporary unpleasantness as par for the course, knowing full well that if they lead their children to discover and do the "should," it's only a matter of time until there will be a reasonable chance they will rise up and call their parents blessed. "Thanks, Mom and Dad, for instilling in us values that last" is about the nicest thing a kid can say and a parent hear.

The Parent's Ultimate Responsibility

To sum up, then, we have to say that the parent has been given an awesome task. If we are going to instill values in our children, we're going to do it by training them in the way they should go, according to divine dictates, by developing practical ways of getting them there, by teaching them behaviors that will adorn their lives with a gracious lifestyle, so that they might discover spiritual realities and avoid destructive behaviors. These are the concerns of a parent who takes parenting seriously.

What kind of learning environment do we need for the kind of development I've just described? Allow me to use a very simple acrostic based on the word *CHILD* that will give us five ingredients necessary for producing an environment in which spiritual learning can take place.

Character
Harmony
Instruction
Love
Discipline

Character

I grew up in wartime Britain. The bombs were falling on us regularly. We would wake up to find entire blocks of houses gone and classmates dead. It was not a secure world for kids trying to grow up. But I remember feeling quite secure. Why? My parents gave me the sense that God would take care of whatever we had entrusted to him. The faith of my father and mother offered to me stability in a frightening, shifting world.

Children are sensitive to the character of their parents. They pick up peace or fear, anger or happiness. And they can withstand a lot of pressure and trial from the outside if the home inside is held steady by parents whose character is steady.

Harmony

We don't need studies to prove to us the damage being done to children by the trauma of divorce. But we might be surprised to learn that children are just as damaged by strife in the home, even when divorce does not occur. It is the responsibility of parents to work out their conflicts for the sake of the children as well as themselves. Children growing up in turmoil will suffer and be hindered in their spiritual, emotional, mental, and even physical growth.

Instruction

> *The wise in heart are called discerning,*
> *and pleasant words promote instruction.* Proverbs 16:21

Note the word *pleasant* in connection with instruction. Children love to learn—they have a built-in desire to accomplish new tasks and gain new skills—but they don't learn well in the midst of criticism and tension. Make learning pleasant as well as instructive for your children. This is part of your task, and it can be one of the most rewarding parts, as you see that son or daughter gain wisdom and apply skill to everyday life.

Love

What more can we say about the importance of love in the home? When we forget the meaning of love, there is always 1 Corinthians 13. An environment that encourages the development of healthy values has a healthy atmosphere of love—kindness, forgiveness, honesty, patience, and so on.

> *Let love and faithfulness never leave you;*
> *bind them around your neck,*
> *write them on the tablet of your heart.* Proverbs 3:3

Discipline

Discipline goes hand in hand with love; one is not complete without the other. How we discipline each individual child varies according to their and our temperaments. But not to discipline your child is a dreadfully unloving thing to do. Our children need to learn boundaries early; they need to see that actions have consequences and that we don't always get what we want or even what is fair. They need to learn how to treat others with respect—and all of this begins at home.

One of the toughest questions parents ask is this: Is there any guarantee that if we do it all right, our children will turn out all right? I don't believe so. There is too much evidence to the contrary—perfectly good parents who have produced kids who are in deep, deep trouble, and perfectly awful parents who have produced wonderful kids.

Jill sometimes reminds me that God had two children, and he put them in Paradise—and they still went wrong. Our children will make their own choices. Our responsibility is to do all we can according to the principles our Lord has given us. In our parenting God never called us to be perfect; he called us to be faithful.

SEVEN

SEX—A DIVINE IDEA

GEORGE GALLUP, after whom the poll is named, has stated:

> There's no question about it, the sex-related issues are
> going to be the most important issues facing all
> churches in the foreseeable future. Abortion, AIDS,
> premarital sex, homosexuality, all those are going to be
> at the vortex.

While we might wonder if this prediction is giving sex more
credit than it is due, we don't have to look far or listen long to
find out otherwise. Recently, as I was driving to Chicago to
speak at a fund-raising banquet for a Crisis Pregnancy Center,
I had the opportunity to listen to afternoon radio, a rare
experience for me. I tuned in to a call-in show, on which a
doctor was dispensing medical advice. The first question came
from a young lady who wanted to get pregnant through artifi-
cial insemination. She was concerned because the proposed
donor of the sperm was an alcoholic. She wanted to know if
her baby would inherit alcoholic tendencies. The doctor asked
why she wanted to be artificially inseminated. He said, "Is your
partner unable to impregnate you?" She replied, "Yes, she's
female." Barely missing a beat, the doctor responded a tad
lamely, "Oh, I see." Further conversation revolved around

complications that might arise because the proposed donor was the brother of her lesbian companion.

The next caller wanted to know if it is possible to contract AIDS through the sperm of a partner who has AIDS and has impregnated you. This led to further questions as to whether there is more danger of catching AIDS through sexual contact alone or through pregnancy.

This enlightening conversation was followed by another questioner anxious to know more about fetal tissue research and what it could do to alleviate Alzheimer's and Parkinson's. What did the doctor think about harvesting cells from the fetuses of elective abortions for the purposes of such research?

Each of these discussions went on for some time, and I wondered if George Gallup was listening. If so, he probably was not as surprised as I was, because he had said that the most important issues out there are abortion, AIDS, premarital sex, and homosexuality. It struck me that the first three questions on that afternoon's call-in show on one of Milwaukee's top radio stations dealt with abortion, AIDS, and homosexuality.

After such heavy subjects we were in for a surprise. The next caller asked about acne. I don't ever remember feeling so relieved to hear a discussion of acne. As the doctor droned on discussing the perils of acne in a tone of voice no different from that with which he had intoned advice on abortion, homosexuality, and AIDS, I realized that nobody had asked about premarital sex, which figured on Mr. Gallup's list. But I didn't have to wait long.

The next program was introduced by the host saying, "Today we're going to discuss the high school student who was chosen by her peers to be homecoming queen." Immediately I knew which high school student he wanted to discuss—the one who was pregnant! When it was discovered that she was pregnant, the administration decided that they didn't want her to be homecoming queen. She was not, in their opinion, a suitable role model for other students. So they rigged the election, covered it up, and the first runner-up was crowned. Somebody, however, spilled the beans, and the guilty parties were fired and the pregnant queen crowned. A considerable degree of outrage was leveled at the administrators who had taken it upon themselves to decide who could and who could not be homecoming queen and who thought they had the right to decide who was or was not a suitable role model. This issue filled another half hour of prime time without difficulty. It also provided the last item of Mr. Gallup's list; premarital sex took its place alongside AIDS, homosexuality, and abortion as suitable fare for afternoon easy listening.

IT WOULD BE A MISTAKE TO ASSUME THAT THIS SEXUAL REVOLUTION ACTUALLY CHANGED SEXUAL BEHAVIOR.

If you happen to listen regularly to radio call-in shows— even those specializing in medical advice—you are probably aware that they have a tendency to be completely sex oriented. But what about the television talk shows? A recent sampling of a typical week's fare turned up the following (the list is not exhaustive—just exhausting):

Jenny Jones
Monday—Women married to transvestites
Tuesday—Maternal incest
Wednesday—Spouses who flirt
Thursday—A girl who sleeps with three stepfathers
Friday—Voyeuristic fantasies

Doctor Dean
Monday—Sex symbols of daytime television
Tuesday—Women and pornography
Wednesday—When relatives fall in love
Thursday—When one man isn't enough
Friday—Nudity

Geraldo
Monday—Inside tabloid journalism (What, no sex?)
Tuesday—Sex scandals in the Roman Catholic church
Wednesday—How a woman can prove her husband is
   cheating
Thursday—Transsexual Tula and her husband
Friday—An exorcism (Not a minute too soon!)

To say that we live in a sex-saturated society is to be guilty of stating the obvious. But sometimes we can be so blinded by the obvious that we don't recognize the environment in which we're living, like many city dwellers who have become so accustomed to smog that they are unaware of the condition of their lungs.

How Did We Come to This?

We can't continue this discussion without remembering something called the "sexual revolution." It reached its peak in those exciting, troubling days called "the sixties." Those were the days when thousands of young people rebelled against most things that their parents stood for—with the possible exception of plastic credit cards—and enjoyed themselves at events like Woodstock. This was a musical event where hundreds of thousands of our brightest and best sang songs of love and peace, sated themselves with uninhibited sex, stoned themselves out of their minds on grass and acid, and slithered in sloppy mud, garlanded in flowers and nothing else.

As I write these words twenty-five years later, many of those young people have grown up to be respectable citizens who listen to music more extreme, do drugs but call them "recreational," and cavort in hot tubs rather than cold mud, while finding ways to enjoy "safe sex." And they have raised kids who in many instances have followed the only role models they had—either their parents or their heroes on entertainment screens or playing fields. And that's how we got where we are.

It would be a mistake to assume that this sexual revolution actually changed sexual behavior. There have always been all kinds of sexual activity, abuse, and aberrations. If you are in any doubt, read the Old Testament; they are all enumerated there quite plainly.

So, if behavior didn't change, how could there have been a

MODERN CULTURE TENDS TO DISPARAGE BEING GOOD AND FREQUENTLY DERIDES GOOD PEOPLE AS "DO-GOODERS."

"revolution"? It was not so much that sexual activities changed, but that attitudes toward these activities changed. There was a time when people, deep down, believed that there was a God who had certain standards. He said, among other things, "You shall not commit adultery," and "You shall not covet your neighbor's wife." This didn't necessarily stop them doing what he had forbidden, but if they did it, they felt that they had done something wrong. So they acted clandestinely. They had to deal with guilt and shame. There was no shortage of shameful activity going on, but at least people had the grace to be ashamed. They had the sense to believe that they were contravening some standards.

But when the sexual revolution came along, attitudes

changed. Instead of having shame placed upon them by society, people were affirmed in their needs and feelings and for their initiative in doing what felt good to them. Behavior that used to be covert became blatantly overt. Historical Judeo-Christian standards of sexual morality were either blandly ignored or boldly repudiated.

From absolutes to relatives

During this time of so-called revolution, attitudes changed drastically where absolutes and relatives were concerned. As in other areas of human behavior, there was a great move away from any sense of sexual absolutes to all kinds of relatives. In the place of a God in whom moral righteousness is found and in obedience to whose principles a morally upright life can be lived, autonomous man was crowned—man who knew better than God how to behave sexually. As God fell out of favor and his righteousness took a tumble, so man took the place of God and decided that what had been regarded previously as naughty was actually nice and what had been off limits was now mainstream. From now on, man would determine for himself what was good and right and true. The net result, of course, is that all kinds of behaviors have become acceptable for the simple reason that people now say, "Nobody has the right to tell anybody else what is right for them. If it is right for you, then it is right."

This is all very heady and high sounding. What could be more adult and mature than the ability to recognize that you don't know everything, that you may be wrong, that other people are as smart or smarter than you are, and that, therefore, the only appropriate way to look at anything is to see it through the lenses of toleration?

Charles Colson, in *The Body*, says, "The only stable value left in this relativistic world is unbridled tolerance. The modern broadmindedness purports that any and all values, if sincerely held, are equally valid (Word, 1992)."

It is not difficult to see that this is a major departure from what the Christian church has believed throughout history. The Christian church does not accept that all standards, if sincerely held, are of equal value. We believe that a person can be sincerely wrong. If there is such a thing as truth, there must, by definition, be something called error. If it is possible to be right, it must be equally possible to be wrong!

From fear to freedom

If there was a move from absolutes to relatives in sexual morals, there was also a shift from an attitude of fear to one of freedom.

Part of our problem is that puberty seems to be happening earlier, and people are getting married later, which means that there is a longer period during which the sexual appetites of young people are developing but cannot be fulfilled legitimately according to Christian teaching. So there is a long, painful period when youngsters are struggling with their sexuality.

When I was in youth ministry (slightly after the medieval period), we found it necessary to talk to young people about sex. In those days our approach was less than sophisticated. We taught them what the Bible says about sex, but we also worked hard to put the fear of the living God in them. We told them about "the three fears": the fear of infection, the fear of conception, and the fear of detection. The fear of infection, stated simply, was, "You don't want to have sex— you could catch a social disease." That's what we called them in those days—"social diseases"—and we never mentioned them by name. This was the "fear of infection." Then we used to tell them, "Listen, you could get pregnant, and then you really would be in a mess. What in the world would you say to your parents? What would they think in your school?" This was the "fear of conception" approach. Now kids can get an abortion without telling their parents, even though they can't have their ears pierced without parental permission! And their schools are so understanding that they will arrange baby-sitting for the children of the children who haven't quite graduated from high school before deciding they are fit to be parents. Warming to our theme, we told the young people of yesteryear, "If you have sex with your boyfriend before you get married, somebody might find out!"— the fear of detection. So the fear of infection, conception, and detection, to a large extent, scared the kids off.

But of course things have changed. Now if you talk to kids about the fear of infection, they look at you as if you just crawled out from under a rock, and they'll bring you up to date on the modern drugs that will handle STDs, which they don't think they will catch anyway. AIDS does scare them a little, but not enough, because they've been indoctrinated about "safe sex," even if they more often than not do not practice it (probably because deep down they have the sense to believe that "safe sex" isn't). As far as detection is concerned, that in their opinion is a "no-brainer." To them it's nobody else's business what you do with your own body. And if anyone objects to your sexual behavior, you can tell him, "Up your nose! Who cares about what you think?" They take comfort in the belief that all those who complain about the decline in sexual mores are probably frigid and frustrated at best and card-carrying hypocrites at worst. As far as conception is concerned, if you are unlucky enough to conceive, then, of course, the ultimate contraceptive, abortion, is available to you on demand. So now the message to our youth is, "Don't worry about infection, don't worry about conception, don't worry about detection. Be free. Don't fear."

Now I will be the first to admit that our old "fear" approach was as subtle as a sledgehammer, but I'm afraid the new "freedom" approach has all the subtlety of the serpent. In matters as deadly—and I mean deadly—as sexual promiscuity, I prefer sledgehammers to serpents.

From being good to feeling good

There actually was a time when people grew up with the desire to be good and to do things that were good. When Queen Victoria was eleven years old, her governess showed her a list of the British kings and queens, and her name was at the bottom. The child burst into tears, then, drying her eyes, stood up and said, "I will be good!" Skeptics would call that kind of attitude positively Victorian! Nowadays she would be surrounded by television crews with reporters sticking micro-

---

EIGHTY PERCENT OF THE
YOUNG WOMEN WHO HAD
SEX BEFORE MARRIAGE
HOPED THAT THEY WOULD
MARRY THEIR PARTNERS.
ONLY 12 PERCENT OF THE
MEN INVOLVED HAD THE
SAME EXPECTATION.

---

phones under her eleven-year-old chin asking, "Do you feel good about being queen one day, Vicky?" She lived in a day when, obvious as it was that she did not feel good about the burdens of royalty, she nevertheless accepted the duties her position had laid upon her—including the duty to be good. How old-fashioned this sounds!

Modern culture tends to disparage being good and frequently derides good people as "do-gooders." To call some-body a do-gooder is something of an insult. The question is no longer, Are there good things that I should do and bad things that I should avoid?; it is, What can I do that will make me feel good? Whether it is good or bad is a matter of fundamental indifference. And if I don't feel good about what I'm doing, then I can always get therapy—therapy that all too often helps people feel good about being bad. This is the way things have progressed.

Now, there's nothing totally new about this. Ernest Heming-way said, "What is moral is what you feel good after, and what is immoral is what you feel bad after." The fact that he eventually killed himself suggests that he finished up feeling as bad as it is possible to feel, and by his own definition his life must have been deeply immoral.

From commitment to enjoyment
Unfortunately, when Christians speak out on matters of sexual morality, people think that they, and therefore God, are against sex. Yet the Bible insists that the first thought about sex was thought by God our Creator. It was God who made male and female for rather obvious reasons. It was he who insisted that people should enjoy sex as an expression of their love and faithfulness. It was his idea that through sex they should pro-duce and then bring up children in the nurture and admoni-tion of the Lord. That is exactly what the Bible teaches about sex in the context of commitment. Somewhere along the line the idea crept in that commitment is the enemy of enjoyment. So it is no surprise that commitment is what people don't want anymore. It is too confining.

Book clubs used to offer free books on the condition that a commitment was made to purchase at least four more books in the following two years. Now they simply offer free books with no strings attached. "No commitment required," they advertise, plastering magazines with our culture's dominant theme! Without commitment, enrollment has boomed. With mandatory commitment it was a bust—because people are looking for enjoyment without commitment, even in the purchase of books!

In the same way, if it is possible for people to have the enjoyment of sex without the awkwardness and the challenge of commitment in which God intended the joy of sex to be experienced, so much the better as far as they're concerned.

The net result of these dramatically changed attitudes is a decisively different atmosphere, an atmosphere in which the message of sex is trumpeted loudly from the rooftops. Sex is fun, sex is freedom, and sex is fulfillment. Tune in to Donahue, Geraldo, Oprah, Sally Jesse, or other talk show hosts, and you will find that the talk often has to do with sex. The more titillating the better. In fact, the producer of one of these shows said recently, "The problem that we're facing now is that there's tremendous competition to get the kind of people on our shows that are going to attract an audience. It used to be if we could get some prostitutes on to talk about being prostitutes, that would do it. But now we have to have prostitutes who love sex, or prostitutes whose fathers approve, because we have to keep ahead of the competition."

Damage Assessment

Even "Dear Abby," who over the years has dispensed a considerable amount of common sense and helpful advice, recently wrote, "Anything that goes on between consenting adults is OK as long as it is agreeable with both parties and harms no one." But former seminary president Robertson McQuilkin, commenting on Dear Abby's tolerant viewpoint, responded, " 'Harms no one' is the key, but who but God knows how much harm is being done?" Exactly! Only God knows how much harm is being done in illicit sexual liaisons, although we can make some fairly accurate observations and do some empirical research as well.

For instance, Dr. Robert J. Collins published in the *American Medical Association Journal* the results of his research on coeds attending midwestern universities. He stated that 80 percent of the young women who had sex before marriage hoped that the premarital sex would lead to marriage with their sexual partner. Eighty percent of them! But only 12 percent of the men involved in the sexual activity had the same expectation—suggesting, once more, that men by nature tend to be more promiscuous and that women have a tendency toward monogamy. Given these widely divergent expectations, who is to say no harm was being done? Who is to say that if a young female student looking for love and relationship and commitment is pressured into a sexual relationship, only to be disappointed in her hopes, there will not be deep, deep harm done to her? And who is prepared to say that the young man, having deceived the young woman and cheated her out of something precious, has not damaged his own credibility and masculinity? If there is any truth at all in the old adage Men give intimacy to get sex, and women give sex to get intimacy, you don't need to have a Ph.D. in psychology to see the possibilities for harm in premarital sexual relationships.

I have been speaking of the potential for harm in premarital sexual activity among college students. But what about the harm done to spouses by cheating partners? Who can measure the sense of betrayal, who can calculate the weight of rejection, who can plumb the depth of pain? Who knows the impact on the bewildered children, and who can calculate the cost of broken homes? Who can estimate the extent of corrupt modeling, and who dares attempt to understand the pain of the Father's broken heart? While our culture trumpets the exhilarating gospel of sex as fun, freedom, and fulfillment, wiser heads shake with dissent, and tender hearts grieve for God's erring children.

One of the most remarkable changes in America's social mores in recent years has to do with changing attitudes toward smoking. Not too long ago cigarette smoking was portrayed on TV as the height of sophistication and an indispensable component of the "good life." Incredibly good-looking young women exuding health and sex appeal elegantly placed cigarettes between their ruby lips and, leaning back languidly, breathed out wreaths of smoke into the sultry evening air. Meanwhile, the Marlboro man, with jawline straight as an arrow and penetrating eyes, gazed from under the rim of his ten-gallon hat intensely into a distance that hinted of adventure. These ads were selling lies. The Marlboro man model, incidentally, was far from healthy; he died of AIDS.

Eventually people caught on. Instead of glamour pictures, someone produced pictures of ashtrays full of twisted, burned, stained, smelly butts. The surgeons general successively added increasingly forthright warnings; the politicians added taxes; and slowly, ever so slowly, the mores changed. People got the message: *We've been sold a bill of goods. Smoking is not what it's been cracked up to be.* And millions saw sense. Now you can't even smoke in many outdoor stadiums. Smoking is outlawed in airports and hospitals. People speak knowledgeably about secondary smoke, and they understand the relationship between smoking and cancer and blood pressure and fetuses. What a turnaround! I look for a similar turnaround in sexual attitudes. We need it desperately. But where to start? It's a matter of values!

EIGHT

WELLSPRING OF LIFE, SNARES OF DEATH

WHAT do Wilt Chamberlain, Magic Johnson, A. C. Green, and David Robinson have in common? Easy! They are all superb athletes who have starred in the National Basketball Association. What do they not have in common? Wilt Chamberlain and Magic Johnson have openly admitted to incredibly promiscuous sex lives, which in Magic's case has led to his contracting the HIV virus. But David Robinson and A. C. Green have made a rap tape on chastity! When A. C. was interviewed by Rush Limbaugh, the hyperopinionated radio personality questioned his message. A. C. simply replied, "I am a virgin!" Limbaugh was finally silenced—a moment to be cherished in the history of radio. But why was Limbaugh silenced? Because it never occurred to him that a young athlete living in the "anything goes" atmosphere of the NBA, where young women make themselves readily available for sex, would choose to be sexually pure. But why would some go the way of a Robinson or a Green and others prefer the path of a Johnson or a Chamberlain? It's a matter of values.

Nothing New under the Moon
Allow me to direct your attention once again to the book of

Proverbs. Chapter 7 specifically. This chapter is unlike many of the other chapters in Proverbs in that it is not a list of apparently unrelated, succinct, pithy, proverbial sayings but is a striking account of a sexual seduction. The story tells of a young man who goes out and is confronted by an experienced woman who leads him into a seductive situation. This is not an antiwoman story. More often than not the sexual aggressor is the male. But in this instance an older woman takes the lead and with much skill offers a young man a tempting opportunity.

There's much that we can learn from this situation. You don't need a vivid imagination to picture the scene:

> *At the window of my house*
> *I looked out through the lattice.*
> *I saw among the simple,*
> *I noticed among the young men,*
> *a youth who lacked judgment. . . .*
> *Then out came a woman to meet him,*
> *dressed like a prostitute and with crafty intent.*
> Proverbs 7:6-10

Notice three specific things. The *vulnerability* of the man, the *availability* of the woman, and the *desirability* of sex. Let me put those three words together and make a very simple equation for you. Vulnerability + availability + desirability = possibility. Possibility of what? The possibility of either doing right or going wrong. The basketball stars I mentioned no doubt have been exposed to precisely the same kinds of situations. The difference, however, between their experiences is simply that two of them chose to do what is right and the other two preferred to do wrong. Every seductive situation offers the chance to go either way. It is worth noting that in the New Testament the Greek word *peirasmos* can mean either "temptation" or "testing." But what determines the difference? Values!

The Heart Is a Sex Organ

Note that the young man in question "lacked judgment." Literally he was lacking in "heart." Now Proverbs 4:23 tells us:

> *Above all else, guard your heart,*
> *for it is the wellspring of life.*

A biblical proverb is a statement concerning the truth that comes from God and that we are to assimilate into our hearts. Truth assimilated then becomes the principle of operation, the standard of values, the basis of lifestyle. The tragedy with the young man in the story is that he lacked heart. He had either missed out on discovering the principles that God has ordained for sexual behavior, or he thought that he knew better

---

THE STORY TELLS OF A YOUNG MAN WHO IS CONFRONTED BY AN EXPERIENCED WOMAN WHO LEADS HIM INTO A SEDUCTIVE SITUATION.

---

than God. What he lacked in heart, however, he more than made up in hormones, and as a result he was a sitting duck. What a sad picture of vulnerability he presents.

Pity many people today who are not only ignorant of biblical principles concerning their sexuality but are constantly exposed to contrary principles. They remind me of one of the most dangerous experiences of my life. As a young marine I joined a number of friends in a sailing expedition for which we were all ill equipped. As a result of our ineptitude, we managed to sail out of sight of land, and when we tried to bring the boat about, we only succeeded in breaking the mast and losing our sails. We were totally lacking in ability to make headway. But it got worse. We then discovered that the tide had turned and was taking us even farther out to sea. So we not only lacked the power to go the right way, even if we'd known which way it was—which we didn't—but we were also subjected to powerful forces taking us the wrong way. We survived, but the survival had little to do with us. We were rescued and towed crestfallen back into port!

But let's get back to our young man. What's happening to him?

> *He was going down the street near her corner,*
> *walking along in the direction of her house*
> *at twilight, as the day was fading,*
> *as the dark of night set in.* Proverbs 7:8-9

If this sounds vaguely ominous, it is. Lacking heart, he's heading in the wrong direction with nothing to hold him, nothing to stay his course.

One day an old gentleman noticed a little boy going round and round the block on his tricycle. This went on all morning, and finally the old man stopped the little boy and said, "Son, aren't you getting tired? You've being going round and round the block all morning."

The little boy replied, "I'm running away from home."

The old man responded, "You're not running away from home, son. You're just going round and round the block."

But the boy insisted, "No, I'm running away from home, but Mommy said I mustn't cross the road."

He was doing what many kids want to do at least once in

their lives—run away from home. Fortunately Mommy had built some boundaries into him. And those boundaries kept him from running into the street. At the moment of vulnerability there were limits that held him, even though he didn't want to be held!

PITY MANY PEOPLE TODAY WHO ARE NOT ONLY IGNORANT OF BIBLICAL PRINCIPLES CONCERNING THEIR SEXUALITY BUT ARE CONSTANTLY EXPOSED TO CONTRARY PRINCIPLES.

But what happens to those who are heading in the wrong direction with nothing to hold them? In their vulnerability they usually meet up with availability dressed up in desirability. And how desirable it is! Those people who say they can't understand the Bible should be made to read Proverbs 7. Language doesn't get much clearer than that.

Macho Man or Sitting Duck

"She took hold of him and kissed him"—hardly the most subtle of approaches. "I looked for you and have found you!" she added. This was heady stuff for a young man on the loose. Flattered, his sense of desirability massaged, his self-image inflated by her attention, what was there to hinder him from responding to her advances?

"Come, let's drink deep of love till morning; let's enjoy ourselves with love!" she said. There was nothing complicated about her approach. She talked about love, but she wasn't interested in love. True love requires commitment and self-sacrifice. She talked of love, but she meant raw sex. And she talked of enjoyment, which was all the young man was looking for. Nothing like a little bit of fun!

Just in case, as a child of the covenant, he had any qualms about doing what the covenant forbade—that is, committing adultery—she told him, "I have fellowship offerings at home; today I fulfilled my vows." He shouldn't have any religious hang-ups, because she was religious, too. She had just come back from the worship center; she had fulfilled her religious obligations, and she had brought back some of the choice meat from her offerings, which meant that there was a steak dinner with the deal. So his conscience could be seared while his steak was grilled. What more could he possibly wish for? Oh, and by the way—her husband was going to be out of town on business for a few days, so there was no need to be afraid. The sex would be safe. No need to be upright and certainly no necessity to be uptight.

"With persuasive words she led him astray; she seduced him with her smooth talk." There is nothing much smoother than the modern offering of sex without shame, without limits, and without consequences. But wait! What is happening to our young friend?

> *All at once he followed her*
> *like an ox going to the slaughter,*
> *like a deer stepping into a noose*
> *till an arrow pierces his liver,*
> *like a bird darting into a snare,*
> *little knowing it will cost him his life.* Proverbs 7:22-23

There's great irony in the way this passage of Scripture ends. Picture the young man, hormones raging, pulse pounding, ego bursting, stepping out to capitalize on an offer that is too good to be true. He's at the top of his game. He's all man, and he's about to prove it. But from heaven's vantage point he looks more like an ox going to slaughter, a deer stepping into a noose, a bird darting into a snare. He's thinking of freedom and fun, but he'll end up fettered by a desire for more and bored by the meaninglessness of his own gratification. Champagne in the evening and real pain in the morning. Or as Carrie Fisher's character in the film *Postcards from the Edge* said with searing honesty: "I was into pain reduction and mind expansion, but what I've ended up with is pain expansion and mind reduction."

> *Her house is a highway to the grave,*
> *leading down to the chambers of death.* Proverbs 7:27

You may say, "That's a bit melodramatic, isn't it?" I don't think so—for two reasons. Number one, the Bible says, "The wages of sin is death." There are all kinds of sin, and sex outside of divinely ordained limits is one of them. Let's be clear about this: The wages of sin is death. So if we're engaging in illicit sex, we need to recognize that we are under the judgment of God, and we should come to repentance, faith, forgiveness, restoration, and newness of life in Christ—and live in purity.

The second thing to bear in mind is this: Dr. J. B. Unwin of Cambridge University studied eighty civilizations that span four thousand years. He concluded, "Any human society is free to choose either to display great energy or to enjoy sexual freedom. The evidence is that they cannot do both for more than one generation." We're dealing not only with sexual behavior that leads to spiritual death and in many instances to physical death, but we're also confronting the possible death of a culture. It's time we took a serious, thoughtful look at our sexual values.

Recognize Seduction's Approach

When cattle smell the slaughterhouse they start to bellow. When deer sense a noose they take to their heels. When birds spy out snares they spread their wings. But the young man in this story does nothing but go right ahead. Why? Because he doesn't understand seduction. Yet seduction is nothing new; there's really no excuse for being suckered. Eve was seduced, of course, but it was all new to her. How exactly was she drawn in?

1. There was a subtle questioning of God's Word: "Did God really say . . . ?"
2. There was a blatant, exaggerated misrepresentation of what God had actually said: "You must not eat from *any* tree in the garden" (italics added).
3. There was an outright contradiction of what God had said: "You will not surely die."
4. There was a distorted representation of the character of God: "God knows it's really like this, but he's telling you differently."
5. There was a lying promise with an overwhelming offer: "You will be like God."

How can anyone guard against such crafty, outright seduction? It wouldn't be difficult to resist if its offers weren't so attractive.

"Has God really said that sex outside marriage is wrong?" has definite Edenic overtones.

"God doesn't condemn sex outside of marriage if you really love each other" smacks of the Garden.

"God knows your sexual needs. After all, he created them. He would want them to be satisfied" sounds like the old serpent.

"Don't worry. You will not be held accountable by God for

your sex life. That's something that priests, puritans, and preachers have dreamed up because they're afraid that someone somewhere might be having some fun" challenges the motives of the clergy but actually contradicts God. Derek Kidner's wise words are worth noting:

> God allowed the forbidden fruit its full appeal. The pattern of sin runs through the act, for Eve listened to a creature instead of the Creator, followed her impressions against her instructions, and made self-fulfillment her goal. (*Genesis,* Tyndale Old Testament Commentary series, Tyndale Press: London, 1967, 68)

Whenever we are confronted with human contradiction of divine principle, to which we respond on the basis of impressions rather than God's instructions because our objective is not to please God but to please ourselves, we are at that moment vulnerable to seduction of all kinds, including sexual seduction. This is an area in which we can see the clear difference between deriving our values from ourselves, our society, or from a sovereign, all-knowing Lord.

Resist Seduction's Attack
Easier said than done! But how?

> *Above all else, guard your heart,*
> *for it is the wellspring of life.*
> *Put away perversity from your mouth;*
> *keep corrupt talk far from your lips.*
> *Let your eyes look straight ahead,*
> *fix your gaze directly before you.*
> *Make level paths for your feet*
> *and take only ways that are firm.*

Do not swerve to the right or the left;
keep your foot from evil. Proverbs 4:23-27

Let me summarize this passage in four basic principles:

- Guard your heart
- Clean up your conversation
- Focus your attention
- Watch your step

Guard your heart

We've already mentioned the crucial role the heart plays, but a couple of things need to be added. If we are to guard the heart, it would be helpful to know "from what?" Among the seven things that God finds "detestable" is a heart that "devises wicked schemes" (Proverbs 6:18). The lady in the story was obviously doing that, and the young man in all probability was doing likewise; why else would he have wandered down to her end of town? If both of them had been careful about the inner workings of their hearts, they would not have finished up where they did. Instead of guarding their hearts they were devising schemes that were immoral and destructive.

Some time ago I was speaking at a pastors' conference. One of the other speakers gave a two-hour lecture entitled "How to Affair-Proof Your Marriage." That it was felt necessary to address this subject at a pastors' conference is surely a sobering commentary on the dilapidated state of some clergy values! I listened with great attention to the information shared with the pastors and then discussed it with a close friend—a psychologist. When I asked him what he thought about the intricate detail of the talk, he surprised me by saying, "There is no real need to go into all that detail. All men need to do is to be strictly honest with themselves. If they regularly check their thought life and are strictly honest about their motives, they will find their behavior appropriate." In other words, "Guard your heart." It's when the heart is given full reign to "devise wicked schemes" that trouble brews. So far, so good, but how are we to guard a heart that has such potential for devising wicked schemes? As we might expect Proverbs has some answers:

> *My son, keep your father's commands*
> *and do not forsake your mother's teaching.*
> *Bind them upon your heart forever;*
> *fasten them around your neck.*
> *When you walk, they will guide you;*
> *when you sleep, they will watch over you;*
> *when you awake, they will speak to you.*
> *For these commands are a lamp,*
> *this teaching is a light,*
> *and the corrections of discipline*
> *are the way of life,*
> *keeping you from the immoral woman,*
> *from the smooth tongue of the wayward wife.*
> *Do not lust in your heart after her beauty.*
> Proverbs 6:20-25

It is important to note that the heart is capable of lusting or listening. It can either allow itself to be captivated by that which seduces to evil, or it can be cultivated by the truth that leads to righteousness. It all depends on the degree of care given to guarding the heart against that which destroys and building it up with that which honors God.

When Paul was trying to help the Corinthian believers as they struggled with the sexual environment of their city, he had some trenchant words to say that bear repeating in our not-so-dissimilar culture. Corinth was the "permissive society" before any such term was coined. One of their favorite proverbs was Everything is permissible, which was a stupid thing to say.

Paul's retort, But not everything is beneficial, was right on target. The Corinthians also said, "Food for the stomach and the stomach for food," which seems harmless enough; but they went a step further and insisted in effect, "Body for sex and sex for body." At that point Paul answered with, "The body is not meant for sexual immorality, but for the Lord, and the Lord for the body" (1 Cor. 6:13).

In other words, he was saying: You can make a logical argument that stomachs and food are made for each other. Stomachs can be regarded as very sophisticated gastronomical machines that process food, turn it into energy, and get rid of the waste. But you cannot project from that, however, that bodies and sex are made for each other, that bodies are sophisticated sex machines. Why? Because while stomachs are designed to process food, which passes away in a matter of hours, bodies are an integral part of a complete person—body, soul, mind, and spirit. If humans are made capable of fellowship with the divine to the remarkable extent of being indwelt by God's Spirit, and the body is part of that humanness, it follows that the body is much more than a sex machine. In fact, every part of a human being has a spiritual dimension, including the body—including sexuality! Therefore, the whole person, including the body, is to be abandoned to the Lord so that the Lord can be abandoned to the body. The body is a temple of the Holy Spirit.

The body, to be understood properly, must be seen not only as something infinitely more complex than a superb piece of physicality but as an integral part of a unique creation designed for divine habitation. And any argument that assumes, for instance, that in the same way that the body gets hungry and thirsty but is satisfied with food and water, so also it gets sexually aroused and should be satisfied with sex, is relegating the body to animal status when it needs to be elevated to temple-of-the-Holy-Ghost status. When these truths are embraced, bound on the heart, fastened around the neck, or however else we want to describe the careful application of truth to life, the result is "the way of life."

But we also guard the heart by protecting it from illicit arousal, from being inflamed. "Do not lust in your heart after her beauty or let her captivate you" is a word for men living in a sex-saturated society. It is perfectly appropriate to recognize beauty. It's perfectly appropriate to appreciate beauty. It is utterly wrong to lust after beauty in the sense of generating such a fantasy desire for it that you wish to possess it.

THERE IS NOTHING MUCH
SMOOTHER THAN THE
MODERN OFFERING OF SEX
WITHOUT SHAME, WITHOUT
LIMITS, AND WITHOUT
CONSEQUENCES.

Now, it's impossible to escape completely from potentially arousing situations or potentially arousing people. Martin Luther had a good point when he said, "I can't stop birds from flying over my head, but I can stop them nesting in my hair." And that's the problem today—too many birds nesting where they don't belong. So we need to remember that there are positive and negative aspects to guarding our hearts. In the positive sense we bind truth upon it; in the negative sense we banish lust from it.

Clean up your language
One of the ways we do this is by recognizing that there is a direct connection between lust in the heart and corrupt talk on

the lips. They feed on each other. Conversation that is unguarded about sexual matters generates lust. Lust in the heart is often spewed out in language, and conversational topics today are full of sexual innuendo or worse. The Bible has a simple rule. It says that out of the abundance of the heart, the mouth speaks. That's why it's so sad to listen to some people speak. What comes out is a reflection of what's inside them. And if their inside is anything like their outside, they have some serious problems. Have you ever noticed how much corrupt talk addresses in demeaning terms such subjects as bodily functions, the opposite sex, and sexual activity? You don't need to think of all the swear words you know, but most of them fit into that category. This is a reflection of commonly held perverted views of the body, sex, and sexuality.

Not only is the word coming out of the mouth a reflection of what's inside, but what comes out of the mouth can negatively affect what is inside. The more we find ourselves enjoying titillating conversation, the more likely our hearts are infected—which is dangerous in a seductive situation. That is why we need to heed the injunction, "Put away perversity from your mouth." That is why we must add "Clean up your conversation" to "Guard your heart."

Focus your attention
"Let your eyes look straight ahead, fix your gaze directly before you." In other words, focus your attention. Job did. He said, "I made a covenant with my eyes not to look lustfully at a girl" (Job 31:1). Too bad David didn't operate on that principle when he saw Bathsheba. Joseph was smarter than David when confronted with the aggressive and available Mrs. Potiphar. He didn't want to focus on what she had to offer; he was more interested in what he was going to do with his life, and he had no time for diversions that were contrary to his divinely ordained goals.

I have often been impressed by the remarkable concentration of big-time athletes. They seem to block out the crowd, the noise, and all other distractions and to concentrate on the game with fierce intensity—"Keep your eye on the ball." They know that the shortest lapse in concentration can result in an error, a fumble, a lost game, even a lost championship.

We need the same kind of keen concentration if we are to maintain our sexual integrity. Our sexuality is so much a part of who we are as persons, and yet it is so easily warped and damaged when we lose our vision of who we are in the divine plan. We are unique creatures of so much worth that God made a way to be eternally connected to us—at great cost to himself. We have the capacity to enjoy the very life of God

> "ANY HUMAN SOCIETY IS FREE TO CHOOSE EITHER TO DISPLAY GREAT ENERGY OR TO ENJOY SEXUAL FREEDOM. THE EVIDENCE IS THAT THEY CANNOT DO BOTH FOR MORE THAN ONE GENERATION."

inside us, to be empowered by the Holy Spirit day by day; yet we so easily relinquish the honor and health of our bodies, which are the temples in which God dwells here on earth.

Sex can become all-consuming, can cause us to wander off the path of our careers, our marriages, and our ministries. Rather than develop the many wonderful gifts of personality and spirit that are waiting to shine through our lives, we squander our energies on immediate physical gratification. We need the concentration of a winning athlete, the dedication of a person who knows where he or she is going in life. That's why I am so encouraged by the A. C. Greens and David Robinsons of this world. Our sexuality is meant to enhance our lives, not consume them.

Watch your step.
Proverbs exhorts us to "take only ways that are firm"—to watch our steps. Now, all this sounds like a lot of rules and regulations. But we must remember that when we come in repentance to God and seek his forgiveness for all manner of sin, including sexual sin, he forgives us for Christ's sake, and he gives us his Spirit. With the life of his Spirit growing in us, we find that our desires will change, and the right decisions will more often seem and feel right to us because our view of life is being transformed. There will always be temptation, but when we begin to experience how rich life can be when lived rightly and purely, our incentive to stay on those "firm ways" will grow.

For now, the rules help us keep to the way that is best for all concerned. Over time, God's law of love will be written in our hearts, and we will feel less and less that external laws are being imposed upon us. Our own desires will equate more and more with what God has been saying and desiring all along. And this, frankly, is what is needed in our society today if people are to live rightly before God in the area of their sexuality. Mere rule keeping will not change the course of society, although it can certainly grant some protection. But true transformation within us, as we discover the high quality our lives can have before a loving God, should be our constant aim.

In conclusion I want to point out that Proverbs is not at all prudish about sexuality. While illicit sex is roundly condemned, the full enjoyment of sexual delight in the context of marriage is unabashedly commended. This should not surprise us, since God invented sex in the first place. Unfortunately, we have to give so much energy to exposing the abuses of this beautiful gift that it is easy for the untaught to gain the impression that sex, of itself, is bad and that God is against it. But we can let go of our hesitancy by meditating on the following.

> *Drink water from your own cistern,*
> *running water from your own well.*
> *Should your springs overflow in the streets,*
> *your streams of water in the public squares?*
> *Let them be yours alone,*
> *never to be shared with strangers.*
> *May your fountain be blessed,*
> *and may you rejoice in the wife of your youth.*
> *A loving doe, a graceful deer—*
> *may her breasts satisfy you always,*
> *may you ever be captivated by her love.* Proverbs 5:15-19

Even the most unpoetic among us can understand that! And it sounds good because it is good.

NINE

WHEN WORK IS WORSHIP,
LABOR IS LIGHTER

GOD intends for his creatures to reflect his own character. This is part of what it means when the book of Genesis says we are made in God's image.

This concept of reflecting God with our lives isn't too difficult to grasp when it comes to what we call "spiritual" issues. But the Scriptures make it clear that we are to demonstrate God's values and characteristics in the more mundane aspects of life also. The values that are found in and emanate from God are intended to be reproduced in all dimensions of life.

It's common to find people who believe in certain spiritual values but keep them in watertight compartments and do not allow them to impinge upon their daily lives. But this isn't the way spirituality was meant to be! True spirituality enters every area of life, giving it newness, energy, and clarity. As we have seen in the book of Proverbs, values that come from God's very character and his purposes for us will make an impact on our marriages, on the way we bring up our children, and on our sexual behavior. These values can also revolutionize the way we see work and approach it.

When we consider that approximately half our waking hours are spent working, it's in our best interests to discover what work is supposed to mean to us! And if we don't have the right values as far as work is concerned, something is sadly out of sync with us during half our conscious living. That should give any living, breathing human pause for thought.

A Careful Look at Ants

Go to the ant, you sluggard;
consider its ways and be wise!
It has no commander,
no overseer or ruler,
yet it stores its provisions in summer
and gathers its food at harvest. Proverbs 6:6-8

It may not have occurred to many of us that the study of the ant should be a priority for establishing our values, but since this passage of Scripture gives us such a clear pronouncement on it, we should at least look into this curious example God has given us.

Sometime when you are out in the woods or in a place where fallen boards and rocks are lying about on the ground, lift one up and take a look. Chances are, there's life under there. And the chances are good that it's ant life. Even a glance at the reaction of a community of ants when their home is disturbed gives us plenty to think about. As we watch them scurry, it doesn't take long to see that there is a method to their scurrying. They are remarkably industrious and organized. They can have all their eggs and other belongings, whatever they are, moved out of sight into underground tunnels in a matter of minutes. Ants and bees are related, so it is not surprising to find that both of them are, if you'll pardon the expression, as busy as bees.

These insects live tragically brief lives (unless they sting or bite you, and then they have lived far too long!), but during their short sojourn they appear to have clearly defined tasks for which they are ideally suited. Sometimes just for a day! Next day they've changed, they have different abilities, they're given an entirely different task, they know what they're doing, they know what they're capable of, they know what they're gifted for, they have an understanding of purpose and objective, and they work hard. All these truths can be learned from ants! The Bible says we should study them and learn from their approach to work.

God works

Fortunately the ant is not the only model of values in the workplace available to us. Right at the beginning of Scripture, where we are told the story of the origins of everything, we are introduced to God without preamble. And what is he doing? He's working! For six intense "days" he works, but "by the seventh day God had finished the work he had being doing" (Gen. 2:2).

> THE FACT THAT GOD WORKS SHOWS THAT THERE IS SOMETHING INTRINSICALLY RIGHT AND GOOD ABOUT WORK.

Now, the fact that God works shows that there is something intrinsically right and good about work. Not only that, when God examined what he had produced through work, he pronounced it good. We can reasonably assume from this that work is fundamentally the right thing for us to be doing. And we are justified in being pleased with the results of work.

People work

Part of what God worked to produce was us! And what did he do with the first human beings? He put them in Paradise.

Paradise! What images that word conjures up for us: Tahiti, where soft breezes lazily stir the thick, green fronds of stately palms, while turquoise breakers roll on white sandy beaches at the feet of dusky maidens bearing cool drinks, which we sip languorously until we drift into relaxing sleep. That, I suppose, is the travel-guide image of Paradise—of Eden. But what did God do with his original Paradise and its original occupants? He put them to work! They were in charge of that vast garden and were to be keepers of the other creatures who lived in it. We were created to *do something*—not to lie on a beach.

But things went wrong. Human beings rebelled against God, and as a result of that their relationship with God, with each other, and with their environment fragmented and fractured. We call this event the Fall. One of the consequences of the Fall, according to Scripture, was that work would be shot through with toil and tedium. So when we find work toilsome and tedious, we're experiencing the consequences of the Fall. These negative aspects that work is so infamous for were completely lacking when the original plan was designed.

Try this little exercise. Imagine doing something you really enjoy doing. Maybe you like to work in the garden. Maybe you're good at crafts, writing, organizing events, talking with people, programming computers, fixing things, or inventing and designing. Imagine doing what you enjoy doing and what you're good at doing—without any backaches, headaches, weeds among the plants, troublemakers among the people, viruses on your computer, and so on. All work is, is doing what you enjoy and what you're good at, and enjoying the results of a day of concentrated work. Sometimes, even after the Fall, we experience days like this—when we work hard and are able to enjoy the results, and we're able to go to bed pleasantly exhausted. This is a taste of God's original intent for our activity on earth. Only after we sinned and were cast from the Garden did the weeds grow and human conflict spoil it all.

Jesus worked

The good news, of course, is that Jesus came into the world to roll back the consequences of the Fall. For thirty years he worked his way through life as a carpenter, then laid aside that occupation and committed himself to a specific ministry. And at the end of this ministry he told his Father, "I have finished the work you gave me to do." It was a work of redemption. He was no stranger to work, whether the dirt-under-the-nails work of a village carpenter shop or the life-draining work of giving fallen people new life.

WHAT DID GOD DO WITH HIS ORIGINAL PARADISE AND ITS ORIGINAL OCCUPANTS? HE PUT THEM TO WORK!

What Can Work Mean to Us Now?

Now, if we can say, as a general rule, that the work of redemption rolls back the consequences of the Fall, it follows that redeemed people may experience a totally new approach to work. They will begin to see work as something that they were created and redeemed to do, and they will embark upon it with considerable delight and great enthusiasm. All this is foundational to our understanding of work, or values in the workplace—our work ethic.

So we have certain models before us of what work is—or what it can be. We've looked at the sovereign Lord and his Son, and we've looked at the Lord's creatures, from the tiny but industrious ant to larger (and less motivated) human beings. But there's more that we can consider.

THE BIBLE STATES QUITE EXPLICITLY THAT HUMAN BEINGS WERE MADE IN THE "IMAGE OF GOD." This highly significant term has been interpreted in a variety of ways. But this statement appears in the context of God, being creative and productive. Those who were made in the image of God at the very time he was in the act of producing them would themselves demonstrate this divine image through creative and productive lives. There's a very real sense in which human beings are uniquely creative and uniquely productive. Granted, beavers build dams, and whales communicate across leagues of ocean, but human beings are obviously in a class of their own. If this is true, then the more creative and productive I am, the more I am fulfilling the uniqueness of my humanity.

Having designated humanity's unique status, God then said that we should exercise dominion over his creation. We were given the responsibility and the ability to move around in the divine creation, to discover its wonders, and to put them to use for the glory of God and for the benefit of humanity. This is something, of course, from which we benefit every moment of our lives.

These words were spoken to unfallen human beings in an unfallen world. Since we know very little about Paradise and human activity at that time, we can only speculate on what this mandate for dominion involved. But we don't need to speculate on what it means in a fallen universe. Left to itself without humans discovering and utilizing its treasures, creation would be nowhere near as wonderful as it is, and life as we now know it would not exist. And as we observe what the abuse of our dominion has also accomplished, it's very clear to us what an awesome responsibility we have been given. Civilization is a direct result of man's creative, productive ingenuity, exercising dominion over that which God has created. But it didn't happen without work.

WHEN JESUS CAME INTO THE WORLD, HE MADE IT CLEAR THAT HE HAD NOT COME TO BE SERVED, BUT TO SERVE. That meant that he had a keen appreciation of human need and that he was absolutely committed to applying himself to meeting that need. He then instructed his disciples to emulate his example and to foster his attitude—the servant spirit. When the servant spirit is channeled into meeting the needs of the world around us, we will work. When we think in these terms, it's easy to see how a servant attitude in the workplace, home, or church that translates into productive, helpful activity will be a mirror of discipleship. Following Jesus means, among other things, doing what he did. Followers of Jesus will be servants, and servanthood involves work.

REDEEMED PEOPLE MAY
EXPERIENCE A TOTALLY NEW
APPROACH TO WORK. THEY
WILL BEGIN TO SEE WORK AS
SOMETHING THAT THEY
WERE CREATED AND
REDEEMED TO DO.

JESUS TOLD HIS DISCIPLES THAT WHEN PEOPLE OBSERVED THE WAY THEY LIVED, THEY WOULD "SEE YOUR GOOD DEEDS AND PRAISE YOUR FATHER IN HEAVEN." In other words, their work would witness to their faith. If you see workers who are aimless on the job, who are careless about their work, and who regard their work as utterly meaningless, you have discovered people who don't have much of a theology of work. They are witnessing to the fact that they're not deriving their values in the workplace from God himself. On the other hand, if you find people who demonstrate in their work habits that they belong to him, you will see the difference in attitude and productivity and will recognize and applaud it—with the possible exception of some workers who prefer not to produce and are shown up by the productive one. In that case the problem is theirs, not the believer's.

GOD HAS CALLED US TO BE COWORKERS WITH HIM. This was clearly the case when God put people in Eden in the first place. The apostle Paul stated specifically that we are coworkers together with God. There are some professions in which it is easier than others to see how we are coworkers with God in fulfilling his purposes, but if we are doing that which we believe God wants us to be doing, then we are working with him in accomplishing his purposes.

I like the story of the pastor who was visiting one of his church members, who happened to be a farmer. After walking around the farm, they took a coffee break. Sitting on the porch looking over the ordered fields, the pastor, waxing spiritual, said, "Isn't it wonderful to see what God has done with his creation?" To which the old farmer said, "It certainly is, and you should've seen what a mess it was when he had it on his own." Now, some people might consider that somewhat sacrilegious, but it is actually quite correct from a theological standpoint. There is a sense in which God's creation is a bit of a mess on its own, but when man comes along as the divinely ordained coworker, it's amazing what can be done. What a wonderful thing it is to go to work knowing that you are cooperating with God in bringing his purposes to fruition!

OUR ULTIMATE MOTIVATION IS TO GLORIFY GOD IN ALL THAT WE DO. Some people work to please the boss; some people work simply to put in the time; some people work in order to get a paycheck; some people work because they just have to work. Often tedium and toil go to work with them each day.

Other people work because they believe that in exercising of their abilities, channeling their energies, and utilizing their time, they are actually glorifying God. They know that they did not create their skills, time, or energy. These are God's gifts, and when we exercise them in appropriate endeavors, we glorify God. When we channel these resources into creative, productive activity that contributes to the community's well-being, we have crowned our work with true glory from heaven.

Earlier generations of believers understood this better than our generation. They used to say, *"Laborare est orare; orare est laborare,"* which means, "To work is to worship; to worship is to work." Try to imagine the factory bench, the kitchen sink, or the storekeeper's counter with *Laborare est orare* written over it. The closest I've come to seeing this is over the kitchen sink in Cliff Barrows's home where the sign "Divine service is conducted here three times daily" is prominently displayed. If

WE MUST ALWAYS REMEMBER THAT WORK AND WORSHIP ARE INEXTRICABLY BOUND UP IN EACH OTHER.

believers went to work on Monday morning with this attitude, not griping like everybody else or simply discussing Sunday football, but applying themselves to work as if it were an act of worship, they, along with their work and the workplace environment, would change dramatically for the better.

Just think of what it would be like in a car pool on Monday morning if the driver greeted everybody with "Good morning—here we go to worship." We must always remember that work and worship are inextricably bound up in each other. Paul told the Colossians, "Whatever you do, whether in word or deed, do it all in the name of the Lord Jesus" (Col. 3:17).

WHEN WE WORK, WE FUNCTION AS PROVIDERS. Paul told the Thessalonians, "When we were with you, we gave you this rule: 'If a man will not work, he shall not eat'" (2 Thess. 3:10). No ambiguity there. It does not say, however, that if a man cannot work he shall not eat. And it doesn't say that if a man cannot find work, he shall not eat. Some people have been very harsh at this point, not understanding the problems of the unemployed or the handicapped. But those who have the ability and opportunity to work and don't are failing to do what they were created to do. Human beings are designed to work in order to provide for their own needs. And not only for their own needs; the Bible also says, "If anyone does not provide for his relatives, and especially for his immediate family, he has denied the faith and is worse than an unbeliever" (1 Tim. 5:8).

That's tough talk by any standards. But it doesn't end there. The Ephesian believers were instructed: "He who has been stealing must steal no longer, but must work, doing something useful with his own hands, that he may have something to share with those in need" (Eph. 4:28).

The thief must be rehabilitated, he must become self-supporting by honest means, but more than that, he must produce a surplus in order that he may provide for the needy. If that is true of reformed thieves, it surely applies to the rest of us. We work not only to support ourselves and those who are dependent upon us, but we work in order to produce value that can then be transferred to people who are in need.

We also work in order to finance the work of the Lord. Now, I'm not going to belabor this point. When we offer to the Lord, as an act of worship, the financial results of our work, that is an act of great value, but more than that, the offering then finances the work of the Lord and brings blessing to others' lives. What a privilege to be able to work at a bench in order to produce value, which in turn becomes an offering in worship, which then brings eternal blessing to someone I will never meet on the other side of the world! Billy Graham used to say, "I can't understand how a brown cow eating green grass can give white milk and yellow butter—but I believe it!" Here's something else that is true, but unbelievable: How can forty hours of digging ditches produce value, which, when it is placed in an offering plate in a church, becomes an act of worship and then finds its way across the seas to a tiny woman living in a squatter camp in Cambodia, making it possible for her to have a roof over her head, food in her stomach, Christ in her heart, and a church in her shack? Tell me that isn't unbelievable. But it's true, and it works when we understand values in the workplace.

TWENTY-SEVEN PERCENT OF THE WORKERS IN THAT PARTICULAR FACTORY SAID THAT UNDER NO CIRCUMSTANCES WOULD THEY BUY THE PRODUCTS THEY WERE MAKING.

Work in Our Culture

But what we've been describing is not the common approach to work in our culture.

A couple of men were working one day. One man was digging a hole and the other man was watching him dig. As soon as the hole was complete, the second man sprang into action and filled it in! A person who was observing said to them, "That's a very peculiar job you're doing. Why do you dig the hole and then fill it in?" The workmen replied, "Well, usually there are three men on this team. The first one digs the hole, the second one plants a tree, and the third one fills it in. But the second guy went deer hunting." This story isn't as ridiculous as it might seem when we take a serious look at many of today's workplaces.

Work as a reason for existing
On the one hand there are those for whom work has become the alpha and omega of their existence. Only in their work do they find meaning. Only in the things that their work provides do they discover personal significance. For them work is not an act of worship unto the Lord. Rather, work is what they worship, and the products of that work are the idols before which they bow. They are not working out of any sense of being created in the divine image or of producing something that will glorify God and benefit the community. They're working because work is their only reason for being, and the money their work provides gives them the things that they crave—the symbols of prestige, the status, the preferential treatment, the shortcuts to where they want to go, the shields against life's unpleasantness. The "best" of everything. It is purely self-oriented, and it often leads them to neglect spouse and family and leisure and worship and voluntary service. Relationships founder, health is jeopardized, and in the end with the Preacher they say:

> *What does a man get for all the toil and anxious striving*
> *with which he labors under the sun? All his days his work*
> *is pain and grief; even at night his mind does not rest.*
> *This too is meaningless.* Ecclesiastes 2:22-23

Work as an imposition to be borne
On the other hand there is the approach to work that perceives it as an imposition to be borne. The attitude is truculent and uncooperative, and the approach is not even close to "an honest day's work for an honest day's pay." It is usually characterized by intense dislike of management on one hand and intense distrust of labor on the other. Bitterness, lack of direction, and laziness are all too apparent when we discuss the workplace with many people today.

I have a friend, a business executive, who has been "let go" three times from three different companies in the space of a few years. In a pastors' conference a number of years ago, I was informed that approximately half of the attendees had been fired by their churches at one time or another, with no recourse and less warning. Managers tell me of employees calling in sick when they are well, taking home what they believe is theirs when it clearly isn't, arriving late, skipping out early—generally ripping off the company wherever they can because they are convinced that they are being ripped off. No wonder there's bitterness! One company went so far as to post this announcement on its bulletin board:

> Sometime between starting and quitting time, without infringing on lunch periods, coffee breaks, rest periods, storytelling, ticket selling, holiday planning, and the rehashing of yesterday's television programs, we ask that each employee try to find some time for a work break. This may seem radical, but it might aid steady employment and assure regular paychecks.

The meaninglessness of work
But many people have a terrible sense of meaninglessness and aimlessness in the workplace. Their work is mundane, repetitive, mind-numbing, cog-in-a-machine, no-sense-of-end-product labor. They are frustrated, watching-the-clock, can't-wait-for-Friday people. And it shows! Daniel Yankelovich reported on research done in one of America's motor industry giants:

> Symptoms of worker frustration were visible everywhere . . . in absenteeism, tardiness, carelessness, indifference, high turnover, the number of union grievances, slowdowns in the periods preceding collective bargaining, and even sabotage. But mostly,

worker frustration was seen in poor product quality
(*New Rules,* Random House, 1981, 43).

Twenty-seven percent of workers in that particular factory said
that under no circumstances would they ever buy the products
that they were making themselves.

According to Scripture, one of the main problems with
human beings at work is laziness. After extolling the industry
of the ant, Proverbs goes on to expose the indolence of the
sluggard. We don't hear the term *sluggard* much anymore, but
it sounds just like some folks.

> *How long will you lie there, you sluggard?*
> *When will you get up from your sleep?*
> *A little sleep, a little slumber,*
> *a little folding of the hands to rest—*
> *and poverty will come on you like a bandit*
> *and scarcity like an armed man.* Proverbs 6:9-11

The sluggard is not painted in very glowing terms here! But
there's more:

> *The sluggard says, "There is a lion in the road,*
> *a fierce lion roaming the streets!"*
> *As a door turns on its hinges,*
> *so a sluggard turns on his bed.*
> *The sluggard buries his hand in the dish;*
> *he is too lazy to bring it back to his mouth.*
> *The sluggard is wiser in his own eyes*
> *than seven men who answer discreetly.* Proverbs 26:13-16

Pictured here is somebody who is committed to procrasti-
nation. Somebody who worships relaxation, who is an expert
at rationalization, and who utterly lacks motivation. A sluggard has little sense of what it really means to be a human being

created in the divine image, possessing latent abilities for creativity and productivity with which to glorify God and contribute to society.

The Difference between Work and Employment

Earlier in this chapter I mentioned a specific problem for the unemployed. Today we find many people who are not working, not because they don't want to, but because there is no work available to them. They are eager to work, but employment opportunities aren't there. It's very easy for them to become discouraged, feeling that they lack significance and that their humanity is being depreciated.

RETIRED PEOPLE SHOULD NEVER GET THE IDEA THAT GOD CREATED THEM TO WORK TILL THEIR LATE FIFTIES OR EARLY SIXTIES AND THEN QUIT.

Let me differentiate here between work and employment. I believe that when there is no employment—that is, work for remuneration—available to us, that does not mean that we cannot work. We should encourage those who are unemployed to find, either inside or outside the community of believers, opportunities to do something creative, productive, and significant, even though they may not receive pay for it. Being unemployed does not mean that a person cannot give an offering to God, care for the family, or help those in need; it merely means that the resource for these activities may not be money. We can still give gifts of our time, talent, and energy.

Retired people should never get the idea that God created them to work till their late fifties or early sixties and then quit. That was never the divine intention. If they are fortunate enough to be in a position to retire, wonderful. This means that they can channel their creativity and the wisdom they've accumulated over the years into new ventures, new personal goals, and new areas of ministry. Retirement should never mean that people stop being creative and productive or that they cease to invest their lives for God's glory and channel their energies to the benefit of the community. What it can mean is that they have more time to do it, and they can do it on a volunteer basis.

When the time comes that there is no need to maintain civilization and there are no more human needs to meet, it could possibly be argued that work will then be unnecessary. Until that day, however, work is in order, and workers are needed. Remember that Paradise wasn't a vacation—it was a vocation.

TEN

MONEY TALKS—BUT
WHAT IS IT SAYING?

MONEY talks.

Loud and clear. What it says is not always pretty.

Take for instance the responses of ordinary Americans to a question posed by researchers working on a book called *The Day America Told the Truth*. The question? What would you do for $10 million?" Twenty-five percent of those who responded said they would leave their families! The same number would leave their church and/or religion, and 23 percent said they would be a prostitute for a week or more. Seven percent were willing to kill a stranger for that kind of money. Apparently values are for sale.

After the survey was taken, the researchers wondered if the $10 million tab had been too tempting. So they asked the same people, "What would you do for $5 million, for $4 million, for $3 million?" The responses were the same. The good news is that at $2 million people began to have second thoughts.

These responses indicate that the way we look at money certainly affects our view of life in general. Or, to put it another way, the value we place on finances can very often be the most dominant of all our values. Economist John Kenneth Galbraith said, "Money ranks with love as man's greatest joy. And it ranks with death as his greatest source of anxiety." Paul expressed similar and even more serious insights when he told Timothy, "The love of money is a root of all kinds of evil" (1 Tim. 6:10). In any study of values, therefore, it is most appropriate to take a careful look at money and our approach to it.

> *In all your ways acknowledge him*
> *and he will make your paths straight.* Proverbs 3:6

"In all your ways" could not be more inclusive! In all aspects of life we are to acknowledge the Lord, and he will act on our behalf. He will make our paths straight. This does not mean that there will be no potholes or roadblocks, but it does mean there will be a clear sense of direction from above in those areas we commit to God.

Money is a very sensitive subject, and we tend to be protective of our resources and defensive when questioned about them. Yet this passage of Scripture goes on to say with inescapable clarity:

> *Honor the Lord with your wealth,*
> *with the firstfruits of all your crops;*
> *then your barns will be filled to overflowing,*
> *and your vats will brim over with new wine.*
> Proverbs 3:9-10

We shouldn't hesitate to see ourselves in these verses just because they use the word "wealth." Most of us certainly don't consider ourselves wealthy. Some of us, in comparing ourselves with our neighbors, have come to the conclusion that we're poor. We don't regard wealth—and proverbs about wealth—as relevant.

However, when compared to the majority of people in our world, any person who can afford to buy this book is wealthy. In fact, compared with people in Indonesia, Laos, Cambodia, and

Vietnam, all of which I have visited in recent years, we are fabulously wealthy. So let's not assume that because somebody next door drives a B.M.W. and we only have a Chevy, this talk of wealth is not for us. Let's not allow such measurements to distract us from the main point of these proverbs. The Lord is to be honored through our possessions, however vast or meager.

TWENTY-FIVE PERCENT OF THOSE WHO RESPONDED TO THE SURVEY SAID THEY WOULD LEAVE THEIR FAMILIES FOR $10 MILLION.

Having said all that, I doubt if there will be many people reading this book who have barns that tend to overflow, but we can still get the point. The Lord was promising his covenant people that the path to general well-being (for them that included being securely established in the Land of Promise) started by acknowledging him—by honoring him. The Hebrew words used in these verses mean to "worship him" or to "esteem him greatly." They were to put the Lord first in their scheme of values, including the way they handled their wealth.

Today we might wonder if a similar principle operates for people whose well-being is not related to living in the Promised Land. I believe that the Lord has given us principles concerning our finances—whether we have much or little, own land or rent an apartment, are direct descendants of the Hebrews or are not even sure who our ancestors are. The Lord knows that money has the power to enrich our lives—or destroy them completely. He has given us guidelines that not only honor him but protect us.

Rich and Poor Have Something in Common

While it is obvious that the circumstances of the ancient covenant people living in the Promised Land were quite different from the situations in which we live today, there are similarities we must not overlook.

> *Rich and poor have this in common:*
> *The Lord is the Maker of them all.* Proverbs 22:2

I am writing this chapter as I sit on the balcony of a twelfth-floor apartment in Caracas, Venezuela. Far below me are well-groomed gardens, shady jogging trails, and inviting swimming pools surrounded by multicolored umbrellas. All around me rooftops are festooned with satellite dishes that reach to the heavens to bring in television programs from around the world. Winding roads are blocked by expensive automobiles. While just across the bustling freeway, perched precariously on steep hillsides are the teeming shantytowns where thousands scratch and scrape for survival in an unforgiving environment, where disease is chronic and crime is ever present. In this place, the rich and the poor live within yards of each other—yet miles apart. Their lots in life have been cast, and the differences are all too obvious.

But these words from Proverbs remind us that people living in entirely different worlds still have the same Maker; they all are created by and for him.

It's My Money

But let's take this a step further. The Lord reminded his covenant people when they entered the Land of Promise that if they became prosperous, they had to "remember the Lord your God, for it is he who gives you the ability to produce wealth" (Deut. 8:18).

This injunction was not limited to the ancient people of the covenant. God still gives men and women the power to produce wealth. When we consider that wealth is related to productive activity, we can't escape the fact that, ultimately, we owe our wealth to the God who gave us the ability, energy, means, and skill to produce whatever has given us our money or our "market value." We can hone our skills, but we can't create them out of nothing. We can use or abuse time, but we can't even stretch it, let alone make more of it. We can place food in our mouths, but we can't create from it the energy that

---

THE LORD KNOWS THAT MONEY HAS THE POWER TO ENRICH OUR LIVES—OR DESTROY THEM COMPLETELY.

---

will stimulate a brain cell, trigger a memory, communicate a concept, or flex a muscle. Skills, time, and energy are gifts. We *are* dependent on the Maker of rich and poor for all that it takes to produce wealth. Wriggle as we might, there is no getting away from it: "It is he who gives you the ability to produce wealth."

There's nothing surprising about the way we struggle with this concept; the ancient Hebrews—the chosen people—weren't too excited about it either! They tended to proclaim, "My power and the strength of my hands have produced this wealth for me" (Deut. 8:17). It was this very attitude that prompted the Lord to remind them that without him there would be no wealth and there would be no work. In fact there would be no "them!" Humbling but true! Paul hit the same note when he asked the Corinthians the rhetorical question, "What do you have that you did not receive?" (1 Cor. 4:7).

But why, if all of it belongs to God anyway, are we required to turn around and "honor" him by giving it back to him?

First, if we see labor (the expenditure of skills, time, and energy) in terms of producing value in the form of goods and services, it follows that value is usually measured in terms of money. The money we amass is therefore an extension of ourselves—our resources, our labor, and what we produce. If we, as created beings, are to honor the one who is our Lord by presenting ourselves in worship, one of the most obvious ways of doing it is in the presentation of the money that is an extension of ourselves. We wouldn't want to chop off a limb and give it or offer our firstborn on an altar, and God obviously wouldn't want that. But since our wealth is an extension of our being as surely as a limb or a child is, God accepts it.

Second, as Richard J. Foster pointed out:

> Money has many characteristics of deity. It gives us security, can induce guilt, gives us freedom, gives us power, and seems to be omnipresent. Most sinister of all, however, is its bid for omnipotence. (*Money, Sex and Power,* Hodder and Stoughton, 1985, 28)

Some of us may be surprised to hear money described as sinister, but we should have no difficulty getting Mr. Foster's point. Money has many characteristics similar to those of deity, and if it isn't handled very carefully, it will establish its reign in our lives. Jesus said, "For where your treasure is, there your heart will be also" (Luke 12:34) and "You cannot serve both God and Money" (Matt. 6:24). But how do we guard against this? By taking steps on a disciplined basis to honor the Lord with our wealth. This will ensure that our wealth does not become our lord.

So we honor God with our wealth because it is an acceptable and appropriate means of offering ourselves, and it is also a practical way of safeguarding against money becoming our god.

If we accept that we should honor the Lord with our wealth, how should it be done? Our concerns divide easily into two categories: how we get money and how we handle it once we've got it.

How Should We Accumulate Wealth?

There is much advice in the book of Proverbs concerning the accumulation of wealth, both positive and negative.

> *Two things I ask of you, O Lord;*
> *do not refuse me before I die:*
> *Keep falsehood and lies far from me;*
> *give me neither poverty nor riches,*
> *but give me only my daily bread.*
> *Otherwise, I may have too much and disown you*
> *and say, 'Who is the Lord?'*
> *Or I may become poor and steal,*
> *and so dishonor the name of my God.* Proverbs 30:7-9

This is an incredibly mature attitude. It recognizes the temptations that either a shortage or an excess of money can bring. It sees honoring the Lord as more significant than making money. It admits to inherent weaknesses of character that need to be disciplined. It testifies to a willingness to be content with life's basics rather than chasing after life's luxuries.

John D. Rockefeller, the multimillionaire, was at least honest when asked, "What else do you want most in life?" His reply: "Just a little more." Most people are critical of this kind of attitude, such as when the professional baseball players, who earn an average salary of $1.2 million, went on strike in 1994. The players were accused of greed and the owners of being just as bad. But given the chance to get "just a little more," how many of their critics would have acted any differently? I came across this anonymous poem some time ago:

Dug from the mountainside
Or washing in the glen,
Servant am I or master of men.
Earn me, I bless you,
Steal me, I curse you;
Grasp me and hold me
A fiend will possess you.
Lie for me, die for me,
Covet me, take me—
Angel or devil
I'm just what you make me.

That's it—angel or devil—and it's just what we make it! Money or wealth can be that which we possess or that which possesses us. If it's the former, it will be a means of blessing. If it's the latter, it becomes a root of all kinds of evil.

Lazy hands make a man poor,
but diligent hands bring wealth. Proverbs 10:4

Once we have adopted an attitude that is aware of money's hidden, seductive powers, we can go about earning diligently and responsibly. The matter of how much we earn has now been placed in the Lord's hands. We've asked him to do the giving as we do the working. Understanding the significance of work (we talked about this in the last chapter, remember?), we now go about our daily tasks, not with a view to making a bundle, but with the intention of working well and accepting what we receive for it as from the Lord. When soldiers asked John the Baptist how they could show they had truly repented, he told them, "Be content with your wages." That's good advice—but how often do we hear anything like it in today's culture?

"There's Danger in Them There Bills"

So we honor the Lord with our wealth by developing positive attitudes toward its accumulation. But we also need to avoid some negatives.

> *The wealth of the rich is their fortified city;*
> *they imagine it an unscalable wall.* Proverbs 18:11

As I look out from my temporary office on this Caracas balcony I can see apartment blocks with security guards, ornately barred windows, double- and triple-locked doors, and every few minutes I hear alarms pierce the air as owners open their car doors and hurriedly unlock their safety de-

---

IT IS NO COINCIDENCE THAT THERE ARE FAR MORE BELIEVERS IN THE BARRIOS OF THE WORLD THAN IN THE UPSCALE NEIGHBORHOODS.

---

vices and disconnect their electronic watchdogs. All in the name of security—and none of it comes cheaply! On the other side of the freeway the people in the barrios have no such luxury; their meager possessions have no such security. Their precarious homes, far from looking like fortresses, give the impression that the next torrential downpour might wash them away. Money buys security. That's the upside. The downside? If money protects you, then the Lord is not necessary. It is no coincidence that there are far more believers in the barrios of the world than in the upscale neighborhoods. Paul was straightforward on this subject when he told Timothy:

Command those who are rich in this present world not to be arrogant nor to put their hope in wealth, which is so uncertain, but to put their hope in God, who richly provides us with everything for our enjoyment.
1 Timothy 6:17

This does not mean that if you can afford it and need it and can stand it, a Doberman might not be a good investment or an alarm system might not help you sleep better. But it does mean that in the end it is the Lord who makes our paths straight. Even the most elaborate precautions money can buy will make no one immune to life's vicissitudes, and even the most expensive investment in personal protection cannot pay dividends of immortality. As Paul said, wealth is very uncertain, and it has a tendency to erode our spirituality.

But if wealth tends to seduce us into trusting it rather than God, it also has the ability to desensitize those who pursue its accumulation. Let's face it—some people make money at other people's expense. One man's profit is another man's loss. There is a perverse law of economics that seems to decree that the rich get richer as the poor get poorer. This may be unavoidable to a certain extent—not being an economist, I don't know— but there's no denying the attitude of insensitivity to others that so often accompanies the accumulation of wealth.

He who oppresses the poor to increase his wealth
and he who gives gifts to the rich—both come to poverty.
Proverbs 22:16

Not everybody is as crass as Marie Antoinette, who, on hearing that the people were out of bread, said, "Let them eat cake." But there is always the danger of a poverty of spirit overtaking a heart of compassion when accumulating wealth becomes a main goal. Wealth can erode compassion.

But there are more dangers in the accumulation of wealth. John D. Rockefeller still wanted more, even though he would have had a hard time spending all his money if he'd wanted to. Money can do that to you. It can create an appetite that resists satisfaction. It wants more—more ease, more security, more

> IF A PROFESSIONAL ATHLETE CONCLUDES THAT THE ONLY THING IN HIS PROFESSIONAL LIFE IS WINNING, HE WILL LIKELY CONCLUDE THAT ANY MEANS JUSTIFIES THIS SOLITARY END.

peace of mind, more prestige, more perks, more status symbols, more toys, more trophies, more of whatever else money can buy. We have to exercise great care to ensure that the pursuit of wealth does not become an all-consuming passion that leaves us spiritually broke, emotionally drained, and relationally bereft. More than one man in his single-minded ambition to climb the corporate ladder has done so rung by rung, only to discover at the top rung that the ladder was leaning against the wrong building. En route he traded his wife, children, health, and friends, and he finished with a sense of loss—a poverty of the soul. Such people would do well to heed Proverbs before it is too late:

> *Do not wear yourself out to get rich;*
> *have the wisdom to show restraint.*
> *Cast but a glance at riches, and they are gone,*
> *for they will surely sprout wings*
> *and fly off to the sky like an eagle.* Proverbs 23:4-5

Or, putting it another way, if less poetically:

That money talks
I'll not deny.
I heard it once.
It said, "Goodbye."

Wealth can erode restraint and common sense. Its accumulation can also erode principle. The legendary coach of the Green Bay Packers reputedly taught, "Winning isn't everything—it's the only thing." Without wishing in any way to suggest that Coach Lombardi was unprincipled in his strategies for winning, we have to be concerned at such an approach. If an athlete arrives at the conclusion that winning is the only thing that matters, then he will also likely conclude that any means of winning justifies this solitary end. Likewise for the equally focused businessman, if making money is the only thing that matters, then principles may quickly fly out the window. Principles of honesty and integrity may be absorbed into "creative bookkeeping"; compassion for struggling competitors may get lost in "dog-eat-dog" philosophy; and shady practice may be excused because "it's a rat race out there." Maybe so—but not everybody has to become a rat.

As the ancient Book reminds us:

One eager to get rich will not go unpunished.
Proverbs 28:20b

So we can honor the Lord with our wealth in the way that we accumulate it. There are right and wrong ways of doing it. The right ways honor God; the wrong ways are destructive to us.

Manage Your Money or It Will Manage You
Now let's turn our attention to honoring the Lord in the way we administer our wealth—however much or little we may

have accumulated. There are three main considerations: establishing sound principles, maintaining healthy perspectives, and developing appropriate procedures.

1. Establish sound principles

Do's and don'ts don't sit well with most people—do they? But we need them anyway. A former youth pastor, when talking to teenagers about sex, would give them the rules: Don't lie down. Don't take anything off. Don't touch below the neck. Not a "do" in sight—but three very good "don'ts." They seemed to serve very well for the traumatic teenage years of raging hormones and confusing signals. He was kind enough, however, to send our son, one of his former students, a cable on his wedding day that said simply, "All three rules canceled."

There is a place for straightforward rules; sometimes we need them to hold us in check until we grasp the larger principles. We hope that as time goes on we will integrate the principles and move on from the rules. When it comes to handling wealth in a God-honoring way, some have grasped and applied the principles, while others haven't learned the rules. Call them rules or principles—whichever suits you best.

DON'T #1: DON'T BUY WHAT YOU CAN'T AFFORD. This can be tough. Advertisers have become so proficient at identifying our insecurities and playing to them that they can scratch us where we don't even know we itch, persuading us we owe it to ourselves to purchase what we didn't know we needed. They know we want to be seen as attractive, to sleep like babies, to live like kings, and to vacation like movie stars. They tell us that the right clothes, the ideal car, the correct address, and the appropriate deodorant will do the trick. Before we know it we're up to our eyeballs in debt, and the advertisers and retailers are laughing their merry way to the bank with money we didn't have. A word from ancient wisdom will help:

Of what use is money in the hand of a fool,
since he has no desire to get wisdom? Proverbs 17:16

An old friend came to visit Jill and me in our home in England. He was a Cambridge graduate, an accomplished athlete, and a potential missionary. But he was strapped for money. He believed the Lord was calling him to Borneo, but he had no way of raising the necessary finances. My wife was consoling him shortly before he was due to leave. As he talked earnestly about his financial problems, Jill introduced a little spirituality into the conversation and assured him that if the Lord wanted him on the mission field, she had no doubt he would provide. Our friend looked out our kitchen window at his shiny red sports car and said morosely, "I think he did—and look what I did with it!" A few minutes later he left our home with a great roar of engine, spinning wheels, and a cloud of dust. Not ten minutes elapsed before he returned, on foot, and sheepishly informed us that he had misjudged the sharp turn over the ancient bridge near our home; one side of the bridge and both sides of his car were no more! There had been some foolish expenditures in his past, but he accumulated a little wisdom en route to the bridge and eventually arrived in Borneo.

DON'T #2: DON'T BORROW WHAT YOU CAN'T REPAY. When I first started to earn my living, I was a banker. In that noble profession I learned some good rules from the banker's point of view. I learned not to lend to people who had inadequate means of repayment. I learned not to lend to people whose assets were less than their debts. I learned not to lend to people whose character had some cracks in it, such as unreliability, untruthfulness, lack of commitment, and laziness, to mention a few. The result was that we had very few bad loans. Business flourished, and everybody agreed that we had a win/win situation.

Somewhere along the line, after I departed the profession, banking took a turn for the worse. (I am not suggesting that there is any connection between my departure and the profession's problems!) Bad debts accumulated, bad loans proliferated, and bad bankers were incarcerated. Sound principles of lending and borrowing were abandoned, and chaos and ruin resulted, from the international banks that folded to people who went bankrupt.

THE CURRENCY OF THIS WORLD IS NOT "LEGAL TENDER" IN ETERNITY.

While I advocate great care in borrowing and lending, I do not subscribe to the opinions of some highly esteemed writers who would prohibit all borrowing. I know that Proverbs reminds us that:

The rich rule over the poor,
and the borrower is servant to the lender. Proverbs 22:7

But that does not put a taboo on borrowing. Scripture does, in fact, endorse borrowing and lending in some instances but warns against usury and the abuse of the needy. So the ancient Israelites were told, "If you lend money to one of my people among you who is needy, do not be like a moneylender; charge him no [excessive] interest" (Exod. 22:25).

DON'T #3: DON'T GUARANTEE WHAT YOU ARE NOT PREPARED TO PAY. Lots of people have been in the embarrassing situation where a friend in great financial straits asked them to stand surety, helping him out of a financial hole. The friend assured them that they only had to sign a guarantee and that would be the end of it. So in good faith they signed on the dotted line. But that was not the end of it, and they were most upset when they were called upon to pay what had been promised. If you are not willing to say good-bye to some of your hard-earned pennies, then heed the word of the Lord:

> *My son, if you have put up security for your neighbor,*
> *if you have struck hands in pledge for another,*
> *if you have been trapped by what you said,*
> *ensnared by the words of your mouth,*
> *then do this, my son, to free yourself,*
> *since you have fallen into your neighbor's hands:*
> *Go and humble yourself;*
> *press your plea with your neighbor!*
> *Allow no sleep to your eyes,*
> *no slumber to your eyelids.*
> *Free yourself, like a gazelle from the hand of the hunter,*
> *like a bird from the snare of the fowler.* Proverbs 6:1-5

There is nothing God-honoring about silly buying, stupid borrowing, or second-guess guaranteeing. There is something honorable about establishing some principles, even if we have to start with elementary do's and don'ts.

2. Maintain healthy perspectives
Bold type grabs our attention, while small print simply strains the eyes. Never is this more true than in the offers of instant riches that find their way into our homes. The dazzling possibilities of living in the lap of luxury, of opportunities that boggle the mind and stretch our horizons, have been known to hypnotize even the most levelheaded person. So much so that the small print never gets read. So let's read the small print; let's make sure we keep a healthy perspective on money. Remember three things:

- Money brings its own problems
- Money has built-in limitations
- Money can't purchase the main things

MONEY BRINGS ITS OWN PROBLEMS. A lot of people believe that a little more money will solve their problems. This may be true, but more money will also introduce some new problems. Getting rid of the old problems may be a relief, but the new problems may be worse than they bargained for.

> *A man's riches may ransom his life,*
> *but a poor man hears no threat.* Proverbs 13:8

I love that one! It's a good news/bad news proverb. First the bad news: "A man's riches may ransom his life." This means that if you're a rich man, somebody may kidnap you. Now the good news: If you're rich you may be able to pay the ransom. The bad news for the poor man is—he's broke. The good news is that he's so broke, nobody is going to kidnap him! So what's better? To be rich enough to pay off your kidnapper or to be so poor that no self-respecting kidnapper would give you a second look? Maybe we shouldn't automatically assume that rich is always better. We shouldn't ever assume that money solves all problems. It doesn't, because it has problems of its own.

MONEY HAS BUILT-IN LIMITATIONS. Here is one of the most chilling, realistic statements on money you'll read anywhere.

> *Wealth is worthless in the day of wrath.* Proverbs 11:4a

It is possible that the day of wrath referred to here is the day of your neighbor's anger. If your neighbor is really mad, your money won't calm him down. In fact, given the love affair with litigation in our culture, it could be that money is not only incapable of assuaging someone's anger but it may even incite him or her to sue you. More likely, however, the day of wrath is the Day of Judgment when the dead, small and great, will stand before God and give an account of their lives. On that great and solemn day money won't help a bit. You will have left it all behind, and somebody else will be thoroughly enjoying it. The currency of this world is not legal tender in eternity. So while financial assets can get you "the best attorney that money can buy," and they can probably get you the best deal the law allows, when it comes to the eternal day in court, money won't help.

MONEY CAN'T PURCHASE THE MAIN THINGS.

> *Better a little with the fear of the Lord*
> *than great wealth with turmoil.* Proverbs 15:16

As we have seen, "the fear of the Lord is the beginning of wisdom." This rule is foundational to the crafting of an eternally worthwhile life. So it is more valuable than anything else in the world. Better to be at peace with the Lord, to have a sense of pleasing and honoring him, and be lacking in financial resources, than to be loaded with assets and bowed down with a crushing load of inner turmoil.

> *A good name is more desirable than great riches;*
> *to be esteemed is better than silver or gold.* Proverbs 22:1

The people of Israel were well aware that their double responsibility was to love the Lord and to love their neighbor. So they understood that life was to be lived on both vertical and horizontal planes. Fearing the Lord was, therefore, quite naturally paired with having a "good name." Today, being respected and seen as people of integrity is still highly significant. Many people do not believe this until it is too late. They are so enamored by wealth and the power and privilege that come with it that they forget to be human and to be concerned about the image they are projecting. Not a few celebrities have found that while their investments were paying great dividends, their stock was taking a beating. There has been a sad procession of the rich and famous who have finished up with resources intact but reputations in tatters.

3. Develop appropriate procedures

Once we have seen that "all that glitters is not gold," we are in a position to handle our resources with common sense, even to the point of establishing procedures that will carry out in practice what we believe in principle. The book of Proverbs is not at all reticent to come up with straightforward instructions.

USING OUR WEALTH IN WORSHIP.

> *Honor the Lord with your wealth,*
> *with the firstfruits of all your crops.* Proverbs 3:9

Those for whom these Proverbs were originally written understood this to mean that they should present their offerings to the Lord in the course of their normal worship experience. They lived in an agrarian culture; their income was tied to their flocks and crops. So as soon as they reaped their harvest, they took the first sheaf to the temple, and there they offered it before the Lord. They took the firstborn of all their flocks to the priests, and they actually committed the firstborn of their children to the service of the Lord.

These were firstfruits. If the Lord is the maker of rich and poor and it is he who gives the ability to get wealth, and if we are to honor him with all that we are, then wealth is part of what we use in expression of our worship. However, as stipulated to the people of Israel, that offering was not to be whatever was left over after they had pleased themselves. In fact, they worshipped God right off the top—with "firstfruits."

USING WEALTH FOR OUR FAMILY. Giving to the Lord must not be at the expense of family. There is nothing God-honoring about a family that is neglected in the name of serving the Lord. He is served in the family as surely as he is worshipped in the sanctuary. So resources properly administered will lead to families adequately cared for.

> *In the house of the wise are stores of choice food and oil,*
> *but a foolish man devours all he has.* Proverbs 21:20

And families are cared for when there is concern for their future as well as their present. This was particularly important for the children of Israel because their continued presence in the Land of Promise was part of God's covenant with them. At any given moment their hold on the territory was tenuous because of the presence of their enemies. So prudent families looked to the future and found ways to make it secure. The modern practice of mortgaging the future is far from biblical and has little to commend it from a practical point of view.

> *A good man leaves an inheritance for his children's*
> *children."* Proverbs 13:22a

USING WEALTH FOR THOSE WHO ARE IN NEED. Taking responsibility for society's less fortunate has always been a prominent theme in Scripture.

> *The righteous give without sparing.* Proverbs 21:26b

> *A generous man will prosper;*
> *he who refreshes others will himself be refreshed.*
> Proverbs 11:25

John Wesley shall have the last summarizing word. He wrote, "Make as much as you can; save as much as you can; give as much as you can." Sorry I didn't say it so succinctly.

ELEVEN

TREATING PEOPLE PROPERLY

SOME books I never start. Some I never finish. Some books finish before I do. But some books I read and reread and refer to often. *Habits of the Heart* falls into this last category. Written by Robert N. Bellah and a group of southern California sociologists, it is the product of their research into American culture. They note:

> For over a hundred years, a large part of the American people, the middle class, has imagined that the virtual meaning of life lies in the acquisition of ever increasing status, income and authority, from which genuine freedom is supposed to come. Our achievements have been enormous. They permit us the aspiration to become a genuinely humane society in a genuinely decent world and provide many of the means to attain that aspiration. Yet we seem to be hovering on the very brink of disaster, not only from international conflict but from the internal incoherence of our own society. What has gone wrong? How can we reverse the slide toward the abyss? (Harper and Row, 1985, 284)

Fundamentalist preachers talk like that quite often, about halting a slide toward an abyss—or words to that effect—but rarely southern California sociologists. But the sociologists went on:

> Our society has been deeply influenced by the tradition of modern individualism. We have taken the position that our most important task today is the recovery of the insights of the older biblical . . . traditions (p. 303).

When I hear that sort of thing, I get excited. But let me back up a little bit and explain to you what they were addressing.

The Makings of a Nation

In the beginnings of American society, there were three central cultural strands, like a rope of three strands. The authors called them *biblical, republican,* and *individualistic.*

Biblical beginnings

The biblical strand refers to the profound influence of such early Americans as the Pilgrim Fathers. They believed fervently in a sovereign God, and they left Europe and came to America believing that they had the opportunity to establish a new society based on biblical principles. One of their leaders, John Winthrop, the first governor of Massachusetts, said, "We must delight in each other, make other conditions our own, rejoice together, mourn together, labor and suffer together, always having before our eyes our community as members of the same body."

These noble sentiments sprang from the Bible, which they loved to read and sought to obey and which they were convinced gave them sufficient information from the Lord as to how to run their lives and their state.

Republican rationales

This second strand referred to by Bellah is not to be confused with the political party. This is not Republican as opposed to Democrat, but rather republican as opposed to monarchist. One of the reasons the colonists left England and came to the New World was that they didn't like living under a monarchy. They were less than enthusiastic about being told what to do by someone whose only authority appeared to be derived from the accident of his birth as the firstborn of his parents—who also had become sovereigns for similar or even less compelling

> ANYTHING THAT PRODUCES A LIFESTYLE THAT BOTH GOD AND PEOPLE ESTEEM HIGHLY IS NOT ONLY UNUSUAL BUT COMMENDABLE.

reasons. Republicans believed that they should be involved in the choice of their leaders.

One of the people who advocated this approach was Thomas Jefferson. He insisted that all people are created equal and that all these people had the right, privilege, and responsibility to be involved in the affairs of society. He even went so far as to say, "Love your neighbor as yourself and your country more than yourself"—a good example of his disconcerting habit of rewriting, amplifying, or editing Scripture to suit his own purposes! So on the one hand there were those who were firmly committed to a sovereign God whose principles, when obeyed, would lead to a healthy society. On the other there were those who believed that every individual should be actively involved in the life of the community and willing to accept responsibility for it.

Individualistic inclinations

Benjamin Franklin was a great example of the much-admired American self-made man, the rugged individual, the one who, born in the land of the free and the home of the brave, had been free enough and brave enough to make something out of his life because he was born in the land of opportunity and made the most of it. Franklin was the quintessential poor boy who made good. Born the son of a soap- and candlemaker, he showed great aptitude in his youth. He became an apprentice in a printer's shop and eventually started his own printing business. By the time he was in his early forties, he had made his fortune and was able to retire and devote his attention to publishing, to writing *Poor Richard's Almanac,* and to scientific experimentation—not to mention, of course, political intrigue and development. This was the man who had taken the initiative and made something of himself. The individualist.

But Bellah points out that there were two entirely different kinds of individualists: those who, like Franklin, were productive or "utilitarian" and those who were like Walt Whitman, the "expressive" individualists. Whitman's individualism was demonstrated in his insistence that he should be perfectly free to be the person that he wanted to be. Nobody else had any right to say how he should live his life, and he seemed to enjoy being a bit of an iconoclast, stepping over accepted norms. He was a free-to-be-me man.

Even a cursory glance at contemporary society will show that the biblical and the republican strands have become severely frayed. The individualistic strand has slipped more and more from the Franklin model toward the Whitman variety, or further from the individual committed to working for the good of society and more to the individual committed to the good of the self. So what is the abyss of which the sociologists were speaking? It is the possibility that our culture may become less and less viable as we lose our biblical moorings, disregard our sense of communal responsibility, and move farther away from a desire to develop God-given abilities, preferring to squander our lives on self-induced gratification.

Some Biblical Values to Stand On

It's not my intention to talk about the political aspects of our situation but to explore what some of these older biblical traditions really are.

Let love and faithfulness never leave you;
bind them around your neck,
write them on the tablet of your heart.
Then you will win favor and a good name
in the sight of God and man. Proverbs 3:3-4

He who pursues righteousness and love
finds life, prosperity and honor. Proverbs 21:21

Notice in these verses the biblical values of love, faithfulness, and righteousness and their end products, which are "favor and a good name in the sight of God and man" and "life, prosperity and honor." Anything that produces a lifestyle that both God and man esteem highly is not only unusual but commendable. And here we see that love and faithfulness result in this kind of approval.

While many people insist on freedom to establish their individual values and others are content to derive their values from community standards, true values are found in the character and nature of God. Love, faithfulness, and righteousness show up consistently throughout Scripture as God reveals his own character to us. These, then, are three biblical values that should be foundational to our personal and community value systems.

Love

The Hebrew word for "love" used extensively in the Old Testament is *hesed*. It has various connotations. It means, first of all, *a steadfast commitment*. Modern notions of love tend to regard it in terms of emotion, but the biblical understanding of love concentrates more on commitment. So the *hesed* of God is a matter of decisiveness—not a warm feeling. The best demonstration of this is in God's decision to make a covenant with the people of Israel. He freely chose to do this, and he took great pains to remind the covenant people that it was not because of who they were that he had been attracted to them and had chosen to place his love upon them. He told them quite bluntly that they were not a particularly winsome or promising group at all. His *hesed* was a matter of what he chose to do and not a matter of what they deserved to receive.

The second characteristic of love, as seen in the character of God, is *a moral obligation to another's well-being*. Over and over again the prophets reminded the people of Israel that God was totally committed and morally obligated to work toward their well-being. Micah the prophet understood this and expressed it beautifully:

> *Who is a God like you,*
> *who pardons sin and forgives the transgression*
> *of the remnant of his inheritance?*
> *You do not stay angry forever*
> *but delight to show mercy [hesed].*
> *You will again have compassion on us;*
> *you will tread our sins underfoot*
> *and hurl all our iniquities into the depths of the sea.*
> *You will be true to Jacob,*
> *and show mercy [hesed] to Abraham,*
> *as you pledged on oath to our fathers in days long ago.*
> Micah 7:18-20

How could God, who had "pledged an oath" based on love, ever renege on his commitment? It was unthinkable. Micah knew that a loving God could be counted on to be "true to Jacob." His love was a moral obligation to follow through on what he had promised.

> THIS KIND OF LOVE IS A STEADFAST COMMITMENT THAT INCORPORATES MORAL OBLIGATION AND THE STRONG INITIATIVES OF KINDNESS, TENDERNESS, AND COMPASSION.

The third characteristic of God's love is *a strong initiative of kindness, tenderness, and compassion.* You may remember that when Moses asked God for a revelation of himself, the Lord said, "The Lord, the Lord, the compassionate and gracious God, slow to anger, abounding in love and faithfulness, maintaining love to thousands, and forgiving wickedness, rebellion and sin" (Exod. 34:6-7).

Love is mentioned there twice in conjunction with such wonderful words as "compassionate," "gracious," "patience" (or "slow to anger"), "faithful," and "forgiving." When you put all those words together, you get a picture of the love of God. Now remember, the point of all this is that we are to pursue righteousness and love. This kind of love! We are not to derive our idea of love from ourselves, nor are we to understand it as portrayed in our society. Love, God's style, has the ability to build up our society rather than tear it down. This kind of love is a steadfast commitment that incorporates moral obligation and the strong initiatives of kindness, tenderness, and compassion. Think of the difference these values would make in today's distressed world. Think of the frayed strands of our cultural rope and see what could happen if we recovered this old biblical tradition.

Faithfulness
Faithfulness, also, is rooted in the character of God. *Faithfulness* is defined as "a determined loyalty to a gracious covenant." Once again we must refer to the covenant God made with Israel. He didn't make a contract. A contract says, "I will do this, and you are required to do that." A covenant says, "I commit myself to doing this. I assume and I trust and I hope and I long for a valid response from you, but my covenant is a commitment of grace, and I will be determinedly loyal to that commitment."

In the book of Lamentations there's a famous phrase, "Great is thy faithfulness," that has been made into a hymn, which we sing with great gusto. Have you ever read that statement in its context? The author of Lamentations—possibly Jeremiah—was deploring the devastation of Jerusalem and the decimation of God's people. But in the midst of his anguish he says:

> *Because of the Lord's great love we are not consumed,*
> *for his compassions never fail.*
> *They are new every morning;*
> *great is your faithfulness.* Lamentations 3:22-23

In other words, he was able to see that even in the midst of unmitigated disaster, they could count on the unchanging loyalty of God toward his commitment. This is the essence of faithfulness.

How many truly faithful people have you known? What kind of difference could it make if you were known to be completely faithful, a person who always followed through on commitments, someone who would rather take a loss or be inconvenienced than go back on his or her word? We live in a society that is shot through with mistrust and fear. We are actually surprised when people do what they say they will do and do it when they say they will do it. If we talk on the phone

---

WE LIVE IN A SOCIETY THAT
IS SHOT THROUGH WITH
MISTRUST AND FEAR.

---

to a person in a place of business, we have learned to get his or her name because we know that when we call again (when what we hoped would have been taken care of hasn't been taken care of), another person will answer, and no one will know what we are talking about. No one is accountable. People are hesitant to take responsibility; they refer us elsewhere or patch us through to the voice mail of someone at another level of the process. And we haven't even touched the area of faithfulness in friendship and in marriage. How refreshing it would be if faithfulness, that old-fashioned biblical value, became valuable to a majority of the people with whom we work and live.

Righteousness

Righteousness in the Old Testament, strictly speaking, means "the fulfillment of the expectations of a relationship." So the righteousness of God is manifested in that, having chosen to make a covenant with Israel, he has always been what you would expect him to be in that relationship or any other relationship that he initiates. So when Moses was getting the people ready to enter the Land of Promise, he reminisced in a song about all the ways that God had dealt with his people in bringing them out of Egypt and leading them through the wilderness. He wrote:

> *I will proclaim the name of the Lord.*
> *Oh, praise the greatness of our God!*
> *He is the Rock, his works are perfect,*
> *and all his ways are just.*
> *A faithful God who does no wrong,*
> *upright and just is he.* Deuteronomy 32:3-4

Notice that Moses, reflecting on years and years of tough living under divine leadership, emphasizes that God has been faithful, upright, and just in all his dealings with the people of Israel. In his turbulent relationship with his truculent people, God had always acted in an appropriate manner. Rightly! His righteousness was evident.

These, then, are the three characteristics of God—love and faithfulness and righteousness—that we are encouraged to develop and display in our own lives as the people of God. It is precisely because these values are rooted in God's character that they are to be reflected in God's people. But what does that mean in practical terms?

How to Put Values into Practice

Acting lovingly

With a bluntness no doubt born of careful observation of human habits, Proverbs states:

> *Many a man claims to have unfailing love [hesed],*
> *but a faithful man who can find?* Proverbs 20:6

Now that is downright discouraging. But it's also very realistic. It is relatively easy for us to proclaim unfailing love—we do it in every wedding ceremony—but it's an entirely different matter for us to produce it. In fact, if the truth were known, we have an inherent inability to produce that kind of love and faithfulness. There is something unloving and unfaithful and unrighteous about us. Nevertheless, there is something in the human heart that longs for love—the kind that is reliable and faithful. The Proverbs say as much:

> *What a man desires is unfailing love [hesed].*
> Proverbs 19:22a

The Revised Standard Version translates the verse, "What is desired in a man is loyalty." When these two possible translations are put together, we can legitimately say that not only can people realistically expect us to be loving toward them but that deep down we want to be that kind of person. But I find a tension within me. I recognize my inherent inability to love that way, but I have a desire to do it, and people desire this kind of love from me. What can I do?

The answer, of course, is that when we begin to recognize our own deficiencies in love and faithfulness, we face up to our failings—our "falling short" of God's standards—and we seek to discover how our sins can be forgiven and our lives changed.

> *He who conceals his sins does not prosper,*
> *but whoever confesses them and renounces them finds*
> *mercy.* Proverbs 28:13

> *Through love and faithfulness sin is atoned for;*
> *through the fear of the Lord a man avoids evil.*
> Proverbs 16:6

There are two things to note here. First, when we operate on divine principles, we will avoid evil. Second, if and when we lapse into unloving, unfaithful, unrighteous actions, we come before the Lord in repentance and seek his forgiveness, and he works a change in our lives. And guess what? We discover that because of his love and faithfulness we now have the power to express love and faithfulness.

> *Those who plan what is good find [or "show"] love and faithfulness.* Proverbs 14:22b

When confronted with our failure, it is very easy for us to simply shrug our shoulders and say, "Well, I'm only human. Everybody else is doing it, and my problems with being loving and faithful are rooted in my childhood, and there's no way I can expect to change at this late stage." But God says, "No! Those who plan to do what is right according to my standards and avail themselves of the spiritual resources I provide for them will find and demonstrate love and faithfulness."

Even as I write this the local papers are full of sickening stories of ten- and eleven-year-old boys murdering old ladies. Of children bearing babies. Children who bear children and children who blow children away—one wonders at a society that has sunk so low that children lack moral sensitivity, qualifying for jail before they have graduated from junior high school. A society where home and family have deteriorated to such an extent that children grow up influenced by all that is evil and corrupt around them rather than by that which is wholesome and healthy. Where the downward drag of sin has no counteracting dynamic to lift young people to higher planes. A culture where leaders bemoan the state of home and family, of inner city and outlying suburb, but appear impotent to bring about change. What's wrong?

Well, that's the question that Robert Bellah and his colleagues asked as they looked at the "abyss." And they knew that a return to the old biblical values was urgently and desperately called for—the reintroduction of God's kind of love. And that doesn't start with a nationwide government-sponsored program; it begins with a revolution of love in my heart and yours.

Acting faithfully

Let me refresh your memory. We defined faithfulness, God's style, as "determined loyalty to a gracious covenant." In our litigious culture, where a woman who spills her coffee over herself not only has the audacity to sue McDonald's but actually wins and walks away a millionaire, we don't think too much of covenants.

WHEN WE OPERATE ON DIVINE PRINCIPLES, WE WILL AVOID EVIL.

We prefer contracts, but contracts that are negotiable if the time comes that we think the contract we freely agreed to is no longer to our advantage. So it is normal for a highly paid athlete to negotiate a contract, find out someone else is earning more, refuse to honor the agreement, and refuse to play until his contract is renegotiated. I'm waiting for the day when an athlete negotiates a contract, has a bad year the following season, and returns his bloated earnings with a note to the effect that he doesn't deserve that kind of money, he hasn't earned it, and it should be given to someone who has produced! And, he would like his contract renegotiated to reflect his lack of production. I'm not holding my breath!

We've all heard of or attended incredibly sentimental, romantic weddings where great promises of fidelity were made only to be broken almost before the ink was dry on the wedding certificate. Some people, wise to that possibility, have shown their uneasiness about the character of the person they are marrying by insisting on a prenuptial agreement that, in effect, invalidates the essence of the vows they are about to take. We have digressed a long way from the basic idea of covenant and therefore from the old-fashioned virtue of faithfulness. Let's take a look at how things could and should be:

> *Like the coolness of snow at harvest time*
> *is a trustworthy messenger to those who send him;*
> *he refreshes the spirit of his masters.* Proverbs 25:13

Here the word *trustworthy* is related to *faithfulness*. There's something refreshing about somebody who promises and follows through. It ought to be so commonplace that it is not so noteworthy, but in a culture where people expect, for very good reasons, to be ripped off, a person who acts upon principles of reliability, trustworthiness, and honesty is unusual.

When Robertson McQuilkin resigned as president of Columbia Bible College and Seminary after his wife, Muriel, was diagnosed as having Alzheimer's disease, he explained that she had cared for him as she had promised; now it was his time to care for her as he had promised. So extraordinary did his action appear, even though it was not at all unusual, given the marital vows they had made to each other long years before, that he was deluged by surprised responses. From Christians! Even the church got a shock when a man did what was right rather than what was easy—for no other reason than he had said he would.

There is an obvious connection between truth and trust and between trustworthiness and truthfulness. Faithfulness is behind all of them. The faithful don't betray trust, and they do project truth. But if breaking contracts has become normative, telling lies has reached epidemic proportions.

> *The Lord detests lying lips,*
> *but he delights in men who are truthful.* Proverbs 12:22

We can realistically expect that faithful persons will be committed to truthfulness, that they will say exactly what they mean, they will mean what they say, and they will stick with it. The Lord delights in this kind of person, which is no surprise since he himself is faithful and truthful. And it is no surprise that he detests lying lips. I think we have to accept the fact that lying has almost become a normative way of doing business. For many people lying is part of the way they relate to each other. Some lie to save another person's feelings. "I just love your dress," they say, when they're thinking, *Why in the world would she wear that?*

More serious is the habit of lying to save your own skin. We learn to do this early on when we tell the teacher, "The dog ate my homework." The practice goes on into high school and college, into job training and business, and into management. Then there's the lie that is told in order to gain the upper hand—the intention is to deceive or to cheat in order to gain something that you do not deserve and in no other circumstances would you ever gain.

The preponderance of lying in our culture was highlighted when *Time* magazine devoted a cover article to the subject in 1992. The article concluded, "Lies flourish in social uncertainty when people no longer understand, or agree on, the rules governing their behavior toward one another. During such periods skepticism also increases; there will be the perception that more people are lying, whether or not they actually are"(5 Oct. 1992, 37).

Whether or not there is a connection between endemic lying and social uncertainty, we'd better get the message that lying is flourishing and "the Lord detests lying lips, but he delights in men who are truthful."

Acting rightly

If we accept the definition that righteousness is the fulfillment of the expectations of a relationship, this gives us lots of scope for evaluating whether we are behaving rightly. But by whose expectations do we evaluate our fulfillment of them? As most of us have found out by bitter experience, you may be able to please some of the people some of the time, but it is impossible to please all the people all the time. Here again our only source must be the sovereign Lord and not our own opinion or a poll of society.

We may be able to convince ourselves that our actions are right because "everybody else is doing it" or because it feels good or achieves the desired objective. But these criteria are not adequate if we have a relationship with God. It is his expectations that really matter.

> *Righteousness and justice are the foundation*
> *of your throne;*
> *love and faithfulness go before you.* Psalm 89:14

Once our righteousness has been established before God by his grace, we embark on a lifestyle of fulfilling his expectations not only in our relationship with him but in all our relationships. Having created us relational creatures in the first place, he also ordained right ways of relating. Scripture is full of information that helps us with our relationships. Marriage and family are two areas in which he has invested particular care and attention. But we have not necessarily approached our family relationships on the basis of what God has designed or expects of us. If we made this switch in our approach to relationships, what a revolution we would see in marriages and families.

In counseling young couples I have found that many of their marital problems stem from unmet expectations. Sometimes the expectations have not been articulated; other times they are totally unrealistic. Expectations can be a minefield because we may not know what they are, but we'll sure know if they aren't met! If marriage and family partners can agree that God's standards and expectations are the right ones, they will establish common ground and will have a much better chance of arriving at a common goal.

I know a young couple whose marriage was in deep trouble. There had been serious failure by both partners. Tempers were frayed, recriminations were flying around, and the possibilities of salvaging anything from a disastrous situation were remote,

---

EVEN THE CHURCH GOT A SHOCK WHEN A MAN DID WHAT WAS RIGHT RATHER THAN WHAT WAS EASY — FOR NO OTHER REASON THAN HE HAD SAID HE WOULD.

---

to say the least. But there was one saving grace. Both parties knew what was right. Some people were encouraging them to do what they wanted; others told them to look out for number one; still others advised them to take each other to the cleaners. But they both knew what was right. And in the end, despite everything else, they made a hard-nosed decision to do what was right. Many of the people who had been involved in the situation were amazed when the couple made a commitment to do what they really didn't want to do, going against the advice of almost everybody. They decided to recommit to each other, to forgive each other, and to do it for no other reason than it was the right thing to do according to their understanding of God's ways.

This works not only in the most intimate relationships but also in the broader spheres of society:

Righteousness exalts a nation,
but sin is a disgrace to any people. Proverbs 14:34

In the complex and perplexing world of politics and states-
manship, it appears that decisions of monumental importance
are often made on the basis of national interest or political
expediency. Even as I write this chapter the debate is raging
over the response of the United States of America to the illegal
regime in Haiti and the actions of Fidel Castro in Cuba. For
some time President Clinton has been threatening an invasion
of Haiti to overthrow the military regime and to reinstate the
democratically elected President Aristide. There are many
people who wonder why we should be bothered with Haiti; it's
not a threat to our security, what they do there is none of our
business, and we shouldn't be putting the lives of young
Americans at risk for the sake of a no-good island anyway.
Others are insisting that we have a moral obligation to see that
democracy flourishes in that nation and to overthrow a violent, repressive regime. Still others are skeptically looking at the
president's abysmal popularity ratings and assuming that he
needs "a little war" to pull the people of America behind him.
But the real question to be answered is, What is the right thing
to do? It is righteousness, not political expediency or national
interests, that our nation must depend on if it is to survive.

Then there's the matter of the Cubans who risk their lives
trying to escape Castro's failed regime by sailing across the
ninety miles of shark-infested waters to Florida on flimsy rafts.
From one point of view, these desperate people should be
helped. But what about the problems faced by the people of
Florida when hundreds of thousands of uninvited people arrive on their shores? And don't forget that the governor is up
for reelection shortly, and his popularity and possible reelection will be greatly affected by how the refugee problem is
handled. The resident Cuban exile population in Florida is

being courted by the president for his reelection campaign, and they are not at all reluctant to let either their interests or their ire be known. So what should the president do, particularly if he wants to see Castro's regime overthrown and doesn't want to help him in any way? And old Fidel is apparently encouraging a lot of the raft people to leave, giving the impression he's glad to be rid of them! So they're probably undesirables anyway! In the midst of all this information there is one question we should be asking: What's the right thing to do?

I have pointed out these current issues simply to illustrate how strange it is for us to think in terms of righteousness. In fact, if we do, we will probably be branded as naive or, worse, "do-gooders." Former president Jimmy Carter, whatever you may think of his political acumen, paid a high price for trying to do the right thing. On one occasion during his presidency, a vote at the United Nations was cast wrongly. The world was startled, but it was obviously a mistake. When the president was informed, he instructed that the mistake should be admitted and the vote recast. His advisers pointed out, however, that the president was being widely criticized at that time for being indecisive—for flip-flopping—and that to change the vote would be political suicide. Better in their opinion to leave the vote alone, even though it was wrong, and ride out the storm. President Carter, however, to his credit—and to his political deficit—insisted that the vote be changed for no other reason than it was wrong. He was committed to doing what was right, not what was expedient. That kind of attitude may have cost him the presidency, but I doubt if it ever cost him a night's sleep.

There is something refreshing about honesty in an age of shady deals. It's always uplifting to hear truth spoken in an environment of lies and half-truths. And there is hope when people do what is right rather than settling for what is comfortable, profitable, or popular. It's that kind of righteousness that exalts a nation.

> *When the righteous thrive, the people rejoice;*
> *when the wicked rule, the people groan.* Proverbs 29:2

Standing for what is right will at times mean taking a stand for justice or taking the part of the underprivileged. In case there's any doubt about this, we need only turn to Proverbs (not to mention many passages in the prophetic books, such as Amos).

> *The righteous care about justice for the poor,*
> *but the wicked have no such concern.* Proverbs 29:7

What this means for the individual who takes the principle seriously will vary from one situation to another. For some it meant being actively involved in the civil rights movement of the sixties, for others it means taking action on behalf of the unborn, while still others throw themselves into relief work for the starving masses of the Third World. But, let's face it—involvement in the cause of justice for the underprivileged is not everybody's favorite pastime.

The more I think about the values of love, faithfulness, and righteousness, the more I am forced to reevaluate my own lifestyle, the more discouraged I become about the contemporary scene, and the more excited I am about the opportunities for radical change if we only dare to revert to the old biblical values.

But how can we do that? The key texts we have been considering talk about three ways of applying this Proverbs wisdom. We are to bind love and faithfulness around our neck and write them on the tablet of our hearts. I've never been that enamored with neckties. However there is no doubt that they say something about the wearer. Whether it is the power tie or the club tie or the psychedelic tie, it makes a statement about the wearer's personality. The same could be said of necklaces that women wear. Whether the fashionable woman who wears a string of pearls with her classic black dress or the artsy one whose neck is adorned by creations that originated in some obscure Indian tribe, both are encircling their necks with statements about themselves. So how about this for a statement? How about moving around on earth wearing a striking commitment to love and faithfulness? That would get noticed in the boardroom and at the cocktail hour, in the sports club and on the family portrait.

IN COUNSELING YOUNG
COUPLES I HAVE FOUND
THAT MANY OF THEIR
MARITAL PROBLEMS STEM
FROM UNMET EXPECTATIONS.

Then there is the picture of writing these values on the tablet of the heart. Paul talked about people's lives being evidence of the effectiveness of the gospel. Picking up on the idea of the commandments being engraved in stone, he said that the Corinthians were "a letter from Christ . . . written not with ink but with the Spirit of the living God, not on tablets of stone but on tablets of human hearts" (2 Cor. 3:3). In the same way that God's commandments given to Moses were put in writing on stone, so also the ministry writes on people's hearts the decision and commitment to "love and faithfulness." And it is there for all to read.

He who pursues righteousness and love
finds life, prosperity and honor. Proverbs 21:21

Whether the thought of pursuit conjures up images of police-men pursuing criminals or hunters chasing deer or even a salesman after a prospect, the common thread through them all is of intense focus and determination. That's what happens when pursuing is the mind-set, and this is a most suitable picture of the single-mindedness that is needed if we are to live in today's scene committed to such values as love, righteous-ness, and faithfulness.

TWELVE

HOW DO YOU SPELL "SUCCESS"?

ON THE strength of the ancient statement "The fear of the Lord is the beginning of wisdom," we have been exploring the idea that wisdom—or, as we might call it today, values—is to be based on a personal relationship with the Lord from whom we come, to whom we go, through whom we live, and unto whom we are accountable. In this concluding chapter I would like to return to this theme, for

> *The fear of the Lord teaches a man wisdom,*
> *and humility comes before honor.*
> *To man belong the plans of the heart,*
> *but from the Lord comes the reply of the tongue.*
> *All a man's ways seem innocent to him,*
> *but motives are weighed by the Lord.*
> *Commit to the Lord whatever you do,*
> *and your plans will succeed.*
> *The Lord works out everything for his own ends—*
> *even the wicked for a day of disaster.*
> *The Lord detests all the proud of heart.*
> *Be sure of this: They will not go unpunished.*
> *Through love and faithfulness sin is atoned for;*
> *through the fear of the Lord a man avoids evil.*
> *When a man's ways are pleasing to the Lord,*

he makes even his enemies live at peace with him.
Proverbs 15:33–16:7

This striking passage begins with a reminder concerning the fear of the Lord and ends with a promise concerning pleasing the Lord. You could say that the fear of the Lord is the beginning of our system of values, and pleasing the Lord is the end that we keep in mind.

The ultimate value for which we should aim, which should be our noble aspiration, is not that we should please ourselves, not even that we should please the community of which we are a part, but that we should be looking to live a life that is pleasing to the sovereign God, who made us.

With that in mind, let me identify for you three ways in which we can please the Lord.

We Please the Lord by Embracing Divine Principles

As surely as there are physical laws in our material world, there are spiritual laws that we ignore at our own peril. There are certain prerequisites to what we like to think of as "the good life." But those prerequisites are surprisingly different from what we might expect. There are many paradoxes in God's divine system of cause and effect. And if we are to enjoy the fulfillment he designed us to enjoy, we will need to understand and apply some universal principles.

Humility comes before honor

One of the most simple but profound statements on the subject of values is, "Humility comes before honor." That is not something that sits well in today's aggressive society, but it is a principle that God has decreed.

It is interesting to remember that the Greeks, who studied virtues at great length, did not include humility in their list of desirable traits. They regarded humility as demeaning, and they much preferred hubris. But the Hebrews did regard humility as a virtue, and later we'll see why.

What does humility really mean? The word *humility* means literally "lowliness of mind." Charles Haddon Spurgeon said that humility is the ability to make a right assessment of oneself. But how do we do this? Paul told the people of the church in Rome, "Do not think of yourself more highly than you ought, but rather think of yourself with sober judgment, in accordance with the measure of faith God has given you" (Rom. 12:3). The operative words here appear to be "more highly," suggesting that it is possible to think highly, not highly enough, or too highly of oneself.

THE THING THAT WE REALLY NEED TO BE LONGING FOR IS THE ABILITY TO SEE OURSELVES AS GOD SEES US.

Robert Burns, the Scottish poet, exclaimed, "Oh would some power the gift give us / To see ourselves as others see us!"

Now, there's no question that the insights of other people can be a helpful addition to our perceptions of self. However, other people have their own prejudices, preconceptions, and problems that may affect the way they see you. Other people's glasses are at best tinted, at worst warped. No, the thing that we really need to be longing for is the ability to see ourselves as God sees us. The extent to which we can do that will determine the degree to which we can gain what Spurgeon called "a right assessment" of self.

Once we think of seeing ourselves as God sees us, we will be well on the road to humility. Why? Because we are God's creatures and he is the Creator. In realizing that we are the created, we must recognize that both our existence and survival depend on our Creator. And if the creature recognizes that he or she has failed to meet certain obligations to the Creator, that creature will experience a sense of having fallen short. If we know in our hearts that we have failed to be all that we were created to be, we will recognize the need to relate not only as creature to Creator but also as sinner to holy God. These insights lead us to humility.

The problem with pride

But why is humility so important? Because it is the opposite of pride. And it is pride that God detests. If humility is lowliness of mind that is appropriate for the creature before the Creator and the sinner before the holy God, then pride is the opposite of an appropriate attitude before God. *Pride* in the Hebrew means literally "a bubbling up or a foaming over." It is the attitude of self-exaltation at the expense of honoring God. Can you imagine anything more fundamentally wrong than exalting self as creature above the Creator? Can there be anything more inappropriate than sinners assuming that they know better than the Eternal One? Pride is offensive to God because it takes us from a place of cooperating in a divine plan to one of fighting both plan and Maker. Ultimately, it seeks equality with God—the sin that transformed Lucifer from an angel to the devil.

Pride is also offensive to God because of its self-preoccupation. Pride regards self as fundamentally more significant than anybody else. When, many years ago, our eight-year-old son and his six-year-old sister indignantly complained to their mother that their four-year-old brother thought he was as important as they were, they could be forgiven for childishness. But the same characteristics in later life would not be as easily forgivable. Then they would have to be called pride. Pride is self-absorbed and denies what God decrees—that I should love God and love my neighbor as myself. C. S. Lewis wrote:

> In God you come up against something which is in every respect immeasurably superior to yourself. . . . A proud man is always looking down on things and people; and, of course, as long as you are looking down, you cannot see something that is above you. (*Mere Christianity*, New York: Macmillan, 1960 paperback edition, 111)

Pride also offends God because of its warped view of the self, which leads to self-delusion. There is no more deluded a person than the one who thinks creature is more important than Creator, sinner more significant than holy God, independence

CAN YOU IMAGINE ANYTHING MORE FUNDAMENTALLY WRONG THAN EXALTING SELF AS CREATURE ABOVE THE CREATOR?

better than dependence, and disobedience more appropriate than obedience. And anybody who believes that fullness of life is found in self-absorption, as opposed to fullness of life being discovered in service to God and to people, is utterly out of touch with the spiritual laws God ordained before time, before human existence.

So we should not be surprised that "the Lord detests all the proud of heart." C. S. Lewis states the case strongly:

The essential vice, the utmost evil is pride. Unchastity, anger, greed, drunkenness, and all that, are mere fleabites in comparison: it was through pride that the devil became the devil: pride leads to every other vice: it is the complete anti-God state of mind (*Mere Christianity*, New York: Macmillan, 1960 paperback edition, 109)

However, if we take seriously this business of pride, if we recognize it in our own hearts and come up with a right assessment of ourselves—humble ourselves before the Lord—he promises that, ultimately, he will honor us.

Take the example of Solomon recorded for us in 1 Kings. Having succeeded David on the throne, he was aware that his father was a hard act to follow and that he had enormous responsibilities to fulfill. He was probably highly relieved, therefore, when the Lord said to him, "Ask for whatever you want me to give you" (1 Kings 3:5). Wouldn't you like God to say that? Solomon's response is very interesting.

> *You have made your servant king in place of my father David. But I am only a little child and do not know how to carry out my duties. . . . So give your servant a discerning heart to govern your people and to distinguish between right and wrong. For who is able to govern this great people of yours?* 1 Kings 3:7-9

There's a lot of humility in Solomon's response, and it was not wasted on the Lord. First he was humble enough to acknowledge God's grace. "You have made your servant king," he says. He did not say, "I am king because I deserve to be, because I've worked hard for it and I am obviously the best choice for the job." He said, "I am king for no other reason than God graciously made me king." He asked for "a discerning heart" so that he might govern the people properly. His response to the open-ended offer to ask for whatever he wanted was clear evidence that he was not in the business of exalting himself. He was eager to receive from God what he needed in order to serve the people. Not only that, he said, "I am only a little child and

> PRIDE IS OFFENSIVE TO GOD BECAUSE IT TAKES US FROM A PLACE OF COOPERATING IN A DIVINE PLAN TO ONE OF FIGHTING BOTH PLAN AND MAKER.

do not know how to carry out my duties"—a statement of his own inadequacy. Solomon is a great illustration for us of humility coming before honor.

Tony Campolo tells the story of the great Florentine preacher, Savonarola, who on one occasion mentioned to a colleague that he'd been very impressed by an elderly lady who prayed fervently every day before a statue of the Virgin. But he was disappointed to be told that there was nothing impressive about her devotion. When she was young, she was very beautiful and had served as the model for the statue. Every day since the statue's erection she had worshiped at its feet. She was not worshiping the Lord or even the Virgin. She was worshiping herself. The ultimate sin is pride. It is fundamentally anti-God and antipeople, and that's why God detests it. If we are truly concerned with pleasing God, we must embrace this principle of humility, of seeing ourselves clearly.

The story is told of Queen Victoria who, at the height of her powers as sovereign of the British Empire, used to attend a

Bible study led by one of her servants—a footman. On one occasion the subject was the return of Christ, and the queen asked the footman when this might happen because she said that she could not wait to lay at Christ's feet the crown of the kingdom and empire. Humility!

Submission comes before success
Recently I had lunch with my friends Jeremy and Heather. He had been successful in business for many years before branching out into a new venture. Heather, who before marriage had been highly successful in the medical field, was thoroughly supportive and encouraging while raising four small children. I had followed their progress with interest and was eager to know how things were going for them. The report was that they had gone through three extremely difficult years, their plans had not come to fruition as hoped, and while their business was looking better than it had at any time, the things they had learned in the three years because of their adversity had been invaluable, and they honestly would not have traded their experience for three years' success in business. In their eyes their three years of disappointing business had been a resounding success. The reason, they explained, was that they had learned about dimensions of life other than material success, that they would not have explored if the material success had been forthcoming. I sensed they were telling me that, having known what it was to be successful professionals, they were getting around to being successful persons. And they liked what they were discovering.

Let's explore this idea of success a little further. Proverbs tells us:

> *To man belong the plans of the heart,*
> *but from the Lord comes the reply of the tongue.*
> *All a man's ways seem innocent to him,*

but motives are weighed by the Lord.
Commit to the Lord whatever you do,
and your plans will succeed. Proverbs 16:1-3

Put those statements together and you come up with something very basic. We make our plans, which may or may not be correct. What determines whether or not they are correct is the

---

PRIDE IS FUNDAMENTALLY
ANTI-GOD AND
ANTI-PEOPLE, AND THAT'S
WHY GOD DETESTS IT.

---

motive behind them. We're not always clear on our motives, but God is, and he evaluates plans on the basis of motives. Therefore, we commit our plans and motives to the Lord and let him evaluate them. And as we do, we can trust him to lead us in the right path—for the Lord works out everything according to his purposes.

So as I look at my life, I make plans and I say, "Here they are, Lord. To the best of my knowledge my motives are right, but you test them, you weigh them; I only want to do what pleases you. I commit my motives and my plans to you, and I ask you to change my heart, to work in my circumstances, to bring about your purposes. And I'll be certain of one thing—if I do that, as I submit to you, I know that you will make my life successful in your eyes."

So humility comes before honor, and submission before success. When we think about these two statements, we can't help but realize how far both are from common perceptions. And we must decide if these are anywhere close to our own perceptions about life. Am I motivated by humility and ener-

CHOICES FOR A LIFETIME

gized by submission? Do I have an overriding concern to please the Lord?

We Please the Lord by Avoiding What He Detests
I've already pointed out that "the Lord detests all the proud of heart." We don't need to reiterate that, but there are other issues related to what the Lord detests that need our careful attention. For example:

> *There are six things the Lord hates,*
> *seven that are detestable to him:*
> *haughty eyes,*
> *a lying tongue,*
> *hands that shed innocent blood,*
> *a heart that devises wicked schemes,*
> *feet that are quick to rush into evil,*
> *a false witness who pours out lies*
> *and a man who stirs up dissension among brothers.*
> Proverbs 6:16-19

The things listed here that God detests all have to do with social relationships.

There are two words to describe these "detestable" attitudes and activities—*competitive* and *destructive.* No doubt a case can be made for the benefits of healthy competition in sports and free enterprise, but there is nothing good to be said for the attitude that drives one to win at all cost, regardless of tactics used or damage done. When skill is pitted against skill so that both are sharpened by the experience, competition achieves something of value for all concerned. And where business competition results in better products at more reasonable prices, the merits of competition are obvious. But when athletic contests degenerate into lies and cheating, violence, and psychological manipulation; and business competition becomes personally, emotionally, and financially ruinous, we must reject it outright. Why? Because from God's point of view, whoever is being unfairly treated, violated, or destroyed is a person of infinite worth. That person, created in the divine image, has dignity and must not be degraded.

Men tend to love a winner. So does God, but he loves losers, too. Particularly, I suspect, the loser who walks away from court bankrupted by the sharp practice of his competitor or

---

MEN TEND TO LOVE A
WINNER. SO DOES GOD, BUT
HE LOVES LOSERS, TOO.

---

the athlete limping away from the jeering crowds and posturing opponents. But surely he delights in those who, touched by the injury of the defeated, choose not to identify with the smirking winners but reach out to the hurting losers, bringing comfort and restoring hope. It is not difficult to understand why God delights in the one and detests the other.

God also detests the kind of spiritual activity that is externally impressive but internally corrupted. For example:

> *The Lord detests the sacrifice of the wicked,*
> *but the prayer of the upright pleases him.* Proverbs 15:8

> *If anyone turns a deaf ear to the law,*
> *even his prayers are detestable.* Proverbs 28:9

The picture here is of somebody who engages in public worship activities, such as prayer and singing, but whose personal life is inconsistent with such activity. The problem is that the worship experience, while purporting to be a reflection of the inner life, is in actuality a carefully crafted subterfuge. It is quite possible that the general public might be hoodwinked into believing that the religious person is indeed a person of spiritual integrity and devotion, but God knows that the religion is less than skin deep and that the things he treasures are being callously abused to the hypocrite's advantage. This in no way pleases or impresses the Lord. It is, in fact, detestable to him.

So if we seriously desire to please the Lord, we embrace what he decrees and avoid what he detests. And he leaves us in no doubt that we should carefully weed out attitudes, social actions, and spiritual activities that he finds utterly distasteful.

We Please the Lord by Doing What He Desires

When I was a boy I tried to do what my parents wished—most of the time! I loved them, but I also knew there would be consequences if I disobeyed. Later in life when I joined the Royal Marines, I tried hard to do what my commanding officer ordered for rather obvious reasons—I had no desire to become acquainted with the "brig," and also for the less obvious reason that I respected him. When I married Jill, I wanted to do what she wanted me to do because I loved her and wanted to make her happy. So for a variety of reasons throughout my life I have tried to do what I ought. But I have to admit that the greatest joy in doing what I ought has always been in bringing pleasure to the one for whom I was doing it.

Let me remind you of the verse with which we started this chapter:

> *When a man's ways are pleasing to the Lord,*
> *he makes even his enemies live at peace with him.*
> Proverbs 16:7

We cannot quote this verse without commenting on the remarkable assertion that the result of pleasing the Lord is a peace pact with the opposition, even though our emphasis is on the first half of the proverb! Remember that this proverb is generally true, but even so, practical experience may leave us a little skeptical of its truthfulness. Look at it this way: If I do things God's way, there is no doubt that my attitudes even

---

SO OFTEN WE ARE RELUCTANT TO HUMBLE OURSELVES ENOUGH TO ADMIT TO THE LORD WHAT KIND OF PEOPLE WE REALLY ARE.

---

toward my enemies will be extraordinary, and that being the case, it is very likely that the opposition will eventually respond with more of a spirit of cooperation than competition. But whatever the consequences may be, we should aim to please the Lord. And he is pleased when we desire what he desires and do what he wishes. Here are three desires of God we can latch onto and practice in our lives.

- He desires that we obtain mercy.
- He desires that we avoid evil.
- He desires that we act honorably.

He desires that we obtain mercy.
After stating, "The Lord detests all the proud of heart" and "They will not go unpunished," it is reassuring to read:

> *Through love and faithfulness sin is atoned for;*
> *through the fear of the Lord a man avoids evil.*
> Proverbs 16:6

The justice of God is, in these verses, married to the mercy of God. For God to be less than just would spell disaster for the human race; for him to be less than merciful would ensure disaster. Fortunately, through his great love and faithfulness, justice has been satisfied in Christ's atonement, and mercy has been extended to the undeserving. God's great desire is that men and women, boys and girls, should avail themselves of the atoning work of Christ that brings forgiveness and reconciliation. And Proverbs reminds us how:

> *He who conceals his sins does not prosper,*
> *but whoever confesses and renounces them finds mercy.*
> Proverbs 28:13

The Lord is delighted when we find mercy through refusing any longer to conceal our sins and freely confessing them. But so often we are reluctant to humble ourselves enough to admit to the Lord what kind of people we really are. The thought of contemplating our own sinfulness is too alarming, the idea of confessing too humiliating, and the thought of receiving mercy too undignified. So we become adept at concealment. We hide sin under pseudospirituality. We bury it under a pile of extenuating circumstances—we were victimized by circumstances or traumatized by environment. We conceal our sin under an impressive display of benevolence and upright citizenship and trust that will be sufficient. But we are constitutionally reluctant to come clean. Our pride gets in the way, our self-sufficiency argues against mercy, and our self-righteousness questions our need of atonement. And all the time the Lord longs for us simply to stop concealing and start confessing. Nothing would please him more.

David, the great psalmist, spoke dramatically about his own experience of "coming clean":

Blessed is he
whose transgressions are forgiven,
whose sins are covered.
Blessed is the man
whose sin the Lord does not count against him
and in whose spirit is no deceit.
When I kept silent,
my bones wasted away
through my groaning all day long.
For day and night
your hand was heavy upon me;
my strength was sapped
as in the heat of summer.
Then I acknowledged my sin to you
and did not cover up my iniquity.
I said, "I will confess
my transgressions to the Lord"—
and you forgave
the guilt of my sin. Psalm 32:1-5

Augustine, the brilliant theologian whose previous life of debauchery had caused him such great sorrow, was desperately conscious of his need for forgiveness and never forgot the wonder of God's mercy. This psalm was such a favorite of his that he had it written on the wall by his bed as he lay dying. His delight in forgiveness knew no limits even then. But while on the one hand the joys of the forgiven are unbounded, on the other hand the delight of the Forgiver knows no limits. Ironically, there are few things that bring more pleasure to God than allowing him to forgive us and show us his mercy. This is what he desires.

He desires that we avoid evil
When evil wears the bloodstained garments of violence or the rags of starvation, it is not hard to recognize or difficult to

reject. But when evil is garbed in the trappings of power or decked out in the finery of sensual gratification, it is much more difficult to avoid. But the Lord desires that we should, nevertheless. And the reason? Because in the end evil shakes the fist in the face of God and wrings the life from the heart of humanity. Attractive it may be, but destructive it will be.

But how can we best avoid the evil that appeals to us? By the "fear of the Lord." This means more than avoiding evil because we fear the Lord's indignation—although this aspect of the fear of the Lord should not be underestimated. But for the earnest believer, judgment—and avoiding it—is not the primary concern. The stronger motivation should be that we are anxious not to displease him by succumbing to evil.

The ruthless tackle by a beaten, dirty athlete may cause lasting damage to a star performer, but when the star avoids the tackle with split-second reflexes and incredible coordination, not only does he protect himself from danger, but he brings delight through his athleticism and grace. Evil is shown to be evil, and grace is shown to be graceful. I sense that the Lord delights in seeing us avoid injury, but he also loves seeing us do it with grace and skill.

He desires that we act honorably
Always in spiritual life God insists that the vertical relationship between himself and humankind be reflected in the horizontal dimension of person-to-person interaction. God is pleased not only by the way we relate to him but the manner in which we respond to people. In fact, the latter is often an indicator of the reality of the former. Proverbs reminds us:

> *The Lord detests men of perverse heart*
> *but he delights in those whose ways are blameless.*
> Proverbs 11:20

Blameless, of course, does not mean sinless or perfect, but it does signify the heart attitude of the person who wishes to live rightly before the Lord in the common affairs of life. The child who respects parents, the adolescent who is responsive to direction, the employee who is reliable and trustworthy, the employer who is fair and concerned, the athlete who plays by the rules, the merchant who regards business ethics, the husbands and wives who are faithful, the politicians who are honest, the attorney who seeks justice, the preacher who proclaims truth, the law officer who is compassionate, the civil servant who serves, and so on. There is nothing particularly

> OUR SELF-SUFFICIENCY ARGUES AGAINST MERCY; OUR SELF-RIGHTEOUSNESS QUESTIONS OUR NEED OF ATONEMENT. THE LORD LONGS FOR US SIMPLY TO STOP CONCEALING AND START CONFESSING.

"out of this world" about the lifestyle that pleases the Lord. How could there be? It's a matter of living by divine rules in human society, of bathing the temporal in the glow of the eternal, and of touching the mundane with the marvelous. And it wonderfully pleases the Lord and becomes increasingly pleasing to those who practice his values.

We have only skimmed the surface of the resources of the ancient book of Proverbs in our search for a system of values— a system based on the character of the sovereign Lord and one to be reproduced in the lives of those who depend upon him and obey him by the gracious ministry of the Holy Spirit. But I trust that we have seen enough to be stimulated to respond to what the Lord says to us about life here on earth in a society being torn apart by competing values. I hope you will find more time to discover more truth and apply it in more ways in your daily life.

EPILOGUE

CHEERFUL GODLINESS

I am writing the final chapter of this book during an all-too-infrequent visit to my native Britain. Between meetings and appointments I relish the opportunity to drink in again the damp freshness of the green countryside, the brilliant blooms of cultured gardens and untamed hedgerows, and the stark contrasts of sun and shade as gray clouds whip across blue skies, driven by relentless westerlies. I revel, once more, in the company of friends rarely seen but whose love has stood the test of decades of enforced absence. And I have been reading again the books of youth and childhood and reliving formative years, among them a selection of Wordsworth's poems, including his lament of England's condition and John Milton's passing:

> *Milton! thou shouldst be living at this hour:*
> *England hath need of thee. She is a fen*
> *Of stagnant waters: altar, sword and pen,*
> *Fireside, the heroic wealth of hall and bower,*
> *Have forfeited their ancient English dower*
> *Of inward happiness. We are selfish men;*
> *Oh! raise us up, return to us again;*
> *And give us manners, virtue, freedom, power.*
> *Thy soul was like a star, and dwelt apart:*

Thou hadst a voice whose sound was like the sea:
Pure as the naked heavens, majestic, free,
So didst thou travel on life's common way,
In cheerful godliness; and yet thy heart
The lowliest duties on herself did lay.

I grew up in the English Lake District Wordsworth knew so well and wrote about so brilliantly, and I have always had a soft spot for his work despite his extravagant romanticism and shaky theology. But on reading his lament for the long-dead old Puritan John Milton, I was struck by the timeliness of what he wrote approximately two hundred years ago, not only for England but for vast reaches of the modern world. There is still a great loss of "inward happiness"—and a desperate, no-stone-unturned search for it. To this day we must admit that "we are selfish men" and are reaping the bitter fruit of it. We need "manners, virtue, freedom, power"—and are not sure where to find them. There is a great deficiency of "cheerful godliness," and we are not even sure that we want something so oxymoronic. In short, we are deficient in values and virtues, sadly lacking in spiritual reality, and desperately deficient in the appreciation of divine grace and mercy, the application of divine principle and decree, and the appropriation of divine power and direction.

We cannot bring Milton or others of his caliber back from the dead, and even if he were miraculously to appear, that would not give us the help we need. But the recovery of the principles he espoused, the values he applied, and the grace he enjoyed would serve to produce again the courage, the cheerfulness, the charity, and the charisma that Wordsworth lauded and England needed. Men and women living such lives "on life's common way" would inevitably turn many others from the jaded paths of self-absorption to the fruitful fields of worshipful service to God and humanity; society would be awakened by splendid lives of high quality flourishing in stark contrast to the sordid behavior so often presented as normative and fulfilling.

But in today's world we do not need romantic poets lamenting long-dead leaders so much as we need ordinary men and women buckling down to the earthly business of deciding if they come from God and go to him, survive because of him and are accountable to him—and if so, whether they are going to abandon themselves to his saving grace in Christ to live under his direction and operate in the power of his Spirit to his great glory.

THERE IS A STILL A GREAT LOSS OF "INWARD HAPPINESS"—AND A DESPERATE, NO-STONE-UNTURNED SEARCH FOR IT.

Should this seem too idealistic, the odds too great, the situation too far gone, perhaps I could encourage you with yet another poem I rediscovered in this nostalgic week—it says a lot to me about not giving up—about believing that there are great possibilities for those who will tackle the task at hand.

Say not the struggle naught availeth,
The labour and the wounds are vain;
The enemy faints not, nor faileth,
And as things have been they remain.

If hopes were dupes, fears may be liars;
It may be, in yon smoke concealed,

Your comrades chase e'en now the fliers,
And, but for you, possess the field.

For while the tired waves, vainly breaking,
Seem here no painful inch to gain,
Far back, through creeks and inlets making,
Comes silent, flooding in, the main.

And not by eastern windows only,
When daylight comes, comes in the light;
In front the sun climbs slow, how slowly!
But, westward look, the land is bright.

—Arthur Hugh Clough
(quoted in *One Thousand Beautiful Things,* ed. Arthur Mee / [Hodder and
Stoughton: London, 1925], 66)

I choose not to accept that, "as things have been, they remain." Even in old England, which leads America by one generation in apostasy, there is an increasing outcry for change among the politicians. The Conservatives tried it but were muzzled when a variety of scandals came to light in their own backyard, and now Labour is trumpeting the call for change in values, led by their new leader. Who knows? Perhaps there is still a chance that the ancient message that "the fear of the Lord is the fundamental basis of a system of values" will get a hearing. But that can happen only as those who know it share the news—and share it winsomely and well.